T<small>AB</small>

D0395536

CHAPTER TWELVE

The Last Word

DEDICATION

To every lady who asked me to write this book
and especially to Sharie, who absolutely insisted.

ACKNOWLEDGEMENT

I shall be forever grateful to Manon
for her endless hours of typing when my arms gave out;
to Gerry at AdVantage Ltd. for her editing and
encouragement throughout the production process;
and to my husband, Paul, who shared both the agony and
the ecstasy of this creation with me.

Testimonials

"Really, how do you know that?"

Those were the most common words uttered by my stepdaughter and I when we spent our first five days in Bermuda. We were on a mission from Canada to find a place to live and an office for the next year or so. We stayed at a "guest cottage" (new words for us) and had lots of tea with Tracey.

She told us about realtors, what type of milk to buy, how the young children packing the grocery bags earn their spending money, how to keep our towels dry. Tracey knew the questions; Tracey knew the answers. Tracey knew we were moving down in the next few months and wanted us to stay here and be happy.

Having spent five years in sales and marketing for many publishers, I thought, here is a great publishing prospect. This woman knows a lot about the island, is eager to share her well-researched information, and can save many families from frustration and added expense if only she were to put it all together in a book. Heck, we would have bought two copies on the spot!

When we returned to Canada to plan our packing and moving, I thought a lot about our teas with Tracey, and from those conversations decided just what type of furniture and clothes to bring. I could start shopping immediately for the essentials of life in Bermuda. I knew what to buy and where to put it before those questions arose.

Now, when we have our friends and family down for a visit and they ask, "How do you know that?", I just smile. People are amazed at just how well I have adapted, but I'm in on the secrets. Life is easier in Bermuda because I know some of the quirks and how to deal with them.

Thank you Tracey and please pass the cream.

Sharie
Canadian

I met a lady in a swimming pool. She was new to Bermuda, the wife of a Bermudian. Her troubles were none too few. In addition to the usual adjustment to life in a new country, she had to adjust also to the responsibilities of running a home – she had always had things done for her. Her misery ran the gamut from feeling unwelcome to feeling occupationally displaced. She had been competent in a job, but now felt drained with no place to lay her burden.

Then she met the author. The author herself was struggling as a new arrival, but found the time to nurture, patiently, her new friend. Today, both women are confident and comfortable with their lives in their new country.

I have seen many people come and go. Some adjust rather easily, some sink into deep depression, but most fall somewhere in between. It can be a very uncomfortable feeling. Wives of foreign workers must carve out a niche for themselves in a society where they have no place outside their circle of family and friends. It is no surprise that many turn to volunteer work (not a bad choice) or excessive sports activity. For those with enough spendable income, there are classes and activities where one can find expression. But, for the career-oriented woman, as well as wives with young children who choose to stay home, there can be many disappointments. I regret to say that, for the expatriate couple, this is often the price to be paid for life in Bermuda. For some it is acceptable; for others it is too high.

I hope that you will find something in this book to provide a source of optimism for finding creative ways to spend your time in Bermuda, be it short or long. There are many opportunities for new growth if one is prepared to accept a new mind-set. And a true Bermudian friend is a delight should you be lucky enough to make one!

Lynn
American

Love takes us to different places in the world. This separated me from my country, my family and friends. As my husband was Bermudian, I had to learn to cope with the lifestyle of the islander. Can a Bermudian understand the difficulties presented to a new-comer to the island? Not unless they have been similarly thrown into a culture that is not their own.

Luckily, I met Tracey. She had arrived a year ahead of me and had already experienced all four seasons. Listening to her experiences helped me to understand and accept the good and the bad of this beautiful island and I am grateful for this.

One day, I was sitting on the couch. Suddenly, I felt a terrible itch-ing. So, I called Tracey. Calmly she told me to get a piece of white paper, put it on the couch and see if tiny, moving spots appeared. They did. She explained these were mites from the sparrow my cat brought in the day before. She then explained how to deal with them. And, that was it! Simple!

Any foreign lady coming to live on this island should read this book. I am certain it will make a difference in her adjustment.

Victoria
South American

Tea With Tracey is one of the most entertaining sources of infor-mation we've ever read. A copy should be made available to all newly arriving visitors and residents on this beautiful island. We think it should be adapted and used in every location in the world! It was especially helpful to us as tourists. You have a winner here – thank you!

Ron & Verrell
Berea, Kentucky

I moved to Bermuda not knowing what to expect. I knew that the pink beaches and the colour of the water were features of this island, but I was not prepared for the everyday challenges that I would be dealing with. Living in this new climate was completely foreign to me.

Fortunately, the first week we arrived, we stayed at Tracey's guest cottage. I spent a lot of time with her getting acquainted with the new surroundings. During this time she helped me adjust to my new country and cope with everything. Her tips on dealing with the humidity, the mildew, the constant cleaning required, the roaches, the ants (and I could go on) has helped me through my stay. I know now that if I hadn't met her, I wouldn't be here today.

The value of Tracey's information cannot be overestimated. If every new resident had the opportunity to spend some time with her, it would save them a lot of time and frustration in adjusting to Bermuda. Unfortunately, she cannot meet every new islander and spend all that time with each and every one. Having read Tracey's book, I know that all the information needed is in it. I recommend this book to any new resident or any lady who wants to know more about this country or, for that matter, every woman who wants to read a good book.

Manon
French Canadian

Introduction

So, you're new here. Sit yourself down; have a cup of tea; I have a few things to tell you. Did you bring your suitcase? This will take about a week.

Let ME tell YOU what happened to YOU. At the point your move to Bermuda was confirmed, your mind filled with a hundred questions. Sure, you had heard of Bermuda but ... well ... it was all ... good stuff. What was the truth? What was NOT in the tourist brochures? What, on earth, were you getting yourself into? Friends and family were no help at all. They just kept "oohing" and "aahing" in envy. You couldn't hold a sensible conversation with any of them anymore. They all sounded like the same recording: Bermuda is beautiful – lush – green – warm; Bermuda is paradise. They were right. Bermuda is all of these. As your well-wishers pointed out, the beauty here is justifiably famous throughout the world.

Crystal-clear waters, pink sands and manicured roads soothe the body and mind. Add to this, low unemployment, an excellent education system (90% of high school graduates go on to further education), sophisticated infrastructure, stable government (a parliamentary system dating back to 1620), friendly people AND no income tax! This is but a sampling of the ... good stuff. You are, *and I mean this*, one lucky lady.

But, alas, nothing is perfect. Those you questioned earlier didn't, couldn't or wouldn't tell you the "real story". I can and I will. My purpose is neither to dissuade you nor to scare you. My purpose is to prepare you. You will have problems – accept that. Even in paradise, there's a price to be paid.

An older Bermudian man (who didn't know me from Adam) stated, "She'll be gone before the year is up." This, in itself, speaks volumes. Well ... give a gal a challenge ....

My first year in Bermuda was a nightmare. I was naïve, wholly unprepared and this was the crux of the entire problem. I wasn't alone. Since then, friends and acquaintances have called me to relate one story after another of those who are "getting on the next plane out of here". They have requested that I intercede and "do something". By then, it's just too late.

By the completion of my second year, there was no question in my mind. Someone had to "do something" for the hundreds of women who were alighting on these shores without the vaguest idea of how to manage the simplest of the nuisances that Bermuda would hand them. WELL, never mind the managing, they didn't even know they would be hit with enough unfamiliar punches to make ANY woman cry. I found my niche! I was ecstatic! I would take these women, one by one, and tell them! What a satisfying job it would be. I would contact every company that was unable to hire enough Bermudians to fill its ranks. I would present my case, with great emotion, to every president who would listen. Most men blatantly admit they do not understand women. I DO! I would save them tens of thousands of dollars! I would assure them that these new recruits would not be forced to pack up and leave because their wives simply could not handle "life in paradise". What a coup!

However, I was not ready for this step. When several women came to me, one after the other, the process was exhausting. It took a week. I lost my voice. I was still discovering and researching and testing this world myself. Who was going to run my house? Could I maintain my enthusiasm relaying the same information over and over again? These and a dozen more questions plagued me. It seemed the process should start in the recruit's home town, BEFORE they got here. I would be away from home for days at a time. After no end of soul-searching, I determined that MY number one priority was MY family and that, no, I was not prepared to shift that emphasis. What I WAS prepared to do though, was to amass all the useful information I could and then, find an effective way to get this information out.

I've learned. And I've found a way to tell you – every one of you. I came up with a new plan. I wrote a book, a preparation guide, the kind of book I wish someone had handed me. The book I *tried* to find … for eight years. Yes, I would prefer to look into your eyes. Everything is in the eyes. But, I can't. Nothing's perfect. Neither am I.

As with all information, it is important to consider the source. I am not an expert on anything; there is no alphabet behind my name. My children often remark that I am prone to exaggeration. I do admit that the temperature has never been either freezing or a zillion degrees. This character flaw can work in your favour – if it sounds worse than it is, you'll be relieved. My friends tell me I'm fussy. Well, yes, I will always turn over an upside down doily. (Why is it upside down in the first place?) We each have our pet peeves. I have many. While I chuckle about a friend's particular list, she chuckles at mine. There is every likelihood that many of the things I find distressing, you won't even notice, or, if you do, they won't bother you in the least. If yours is a two-year contract, many of these matters will not have time to touch you. However, contracts can be renewed for decades; you may not want to go home when the time comes. Or, if you have married a Bermudian, you could be here for a long, long time.

I am assuming I'm having tea with a female. This (as the back cover illustrates) is not to dismiss men. We have operated a small guest house for more than a decade now. About half of our clients are companies that place new employees with us while they find a permanent home. For the most part, these new hires are men. I've spent *many hours* empathizing with men. It's just that, never having been a man myself, I don't feel properly qualified to speak on their behalf. But, I will make one comment. Men deal with life on a global scale – curtains on the windows is neither here nor there, but a woman *must* have her nest in order. It's instinctive. If you, dear reader, are male, I entreat you to *keep your nest in order.* Untidy, in Bermuda, sets the stage for destruction. This is covered extensively in the pages to follow.

I promise: This book will help you, it will save you from the "Tough Morning", it will save you tears. It just doesn't make sense for each and every one of you to spend YEARS haphazardly accumulating the same information I am happy to share with you now.

Tracey
Spring 1994

Wow, a second printing and now, a second edition! Who'd have thought? Anything is possible. This includes the painting of the ENTIRE *Tea with Tracey* cover on an acrylic fingernail. I'm not kidding. Shortly after the book hit the shelves, a reader knocked on my door and presented me with this work of art. To call forth this type of talent – another unexpected reward.

Thank you, dear readers, for your letters and e-mails and cards and calls. Thank you for the hugs and handshakes. It has been an incredible experience – a true life event. Thank you for helping me show there was a need.

It is now time for an update. Here it is with additions that have often been requested. Hoping this helps even more ....

Tracey
Summer 2003

TOUGH MORNING

It had been a tough morning. I awoke covered in damp bed-clothes, stepped onto a damp rug, dressed in damp clothes and walked into the kitchen. The counters and table were covered with droplets of some sort of liquid. Now, what's this all about?, I thought. It was 100% humidity; it was raining, IN my house!

I thought, well, never mind, just get on with the day's work and ignore it. But, I COULDN'T wash the floors (how would they dry?), I COULDN'T make the cake (it would fall upon removal from the oven), I COULDN'T vacuum (that machine is not made to be pushed around wet rugs).

So, I thought, well, never mind, I'll spend the day writing letters. The paper was damp; the ink smeared, but I did get a letter written. However, when I went to put it in the envelope, I found all 250 of my new envelopes had self-sealed. The humidity had done this for me. Okay, I thought, just calm down, have a cigarette (I was a smoker then!) and ponder these problems one by one. My matches wouldn't light; they too were wet.

So, I thought, well, never mind, I'll spend the day on myself. My shaver dragged on my damp skin, my nail polish would NOT dry, my mascara ended up on my cheeks. I curled my hair; that lasted ten minutes. Now, I was getting a bit cranky.

So, I thought, *just relax*, sit down and have a bowl of cereal. There were ants in the cereal. "ALL RIGHT, FINE," I announced to no one in particular, "I'll have a couple of pieces of toast." I took the butter dish out of the cupboard. A blood-curdling scream ripped from my body. I threw the dish (coating the walls, ceiling, cupboards and floor with butter) and ran out of the kitchen on jelly-like legs. Spread-eagled across the full diameter of the butter dish was a huge, black cockroach!

It was noon. I sat in the middle of the living room floor and cried.

CHAPTER ONE

*'Tis the
Season for Survival*

HUMIDITY

Humidity is the instigator of a zillion problems. I blame every-thing on humidity. Well ... it just seems as though, either directly or indirectly, this is the culprit behind so many frustrations. Just as water is a key ingredient for life, water in the air (and lots of it) serves as a catalyst for the multiplication of every life form known to man! The bugs and spores and seeds are present always. In a dormant state, this is not a problem. However, given the right conditions (humidity being paramount), mould, mildew, rust, bugs, dampness, rot and odours thrive unchecked. The lowest air over oceans is almost always saturated. On an island, in many places barely a mile wide, guess where that leaves us?

For those born in tropical climes, it is next to impossible to believe that man can survive through a winter of 30 below zero tem-peratures; that a radio announcement will caution, "Exposed skin will freeze in four minutes." However, for this native prairie girl, it's pretty mundane stuff – it's winter. This is not a problem. Man, blessed with the power to reason, finds a route over every mountain, taking the necessary steps and precautions to survive and (yes!) enjoy this minor nuisance. To prairie people, it is inconceivable that 60 degrees could, by any stretch of the imagination, be considered cold or that 85 could be too hot. They, of course, have no conception of the power of humidity.

Humidity makes the summers hot, the winters cold. For those of you from the colder climes, let me explain it in terms of wind chill. Dressed appropriately, 20 below zero is not a problem, but, if a gale is blowing, it is so cold that your very survival is at stake. Humidity fol-lows this pattern. Warm becomes hot; cool becomes cold. As humid-ity rises, evaporation slows. In summer, slow evaporation leaves us perspiration-soaked and hot; in winter, damp clothing on a cool day ensures one cold body. The body's natural defense system of tem-perature control (perspiration and evaporation) is short-circuited.

Humidity makes food soggy. Crackers, cookies, potato chips or anything that should crunch, won't, in high humidity. Sugar, salt, crystals and powders of all sorts absorb this moisture in the air and become one large lump. A granule of instant coffee left on the counter becomes a stain. Solve these problems by keeping dry foods, powders, crystals and salts in the fridge. (No, rice in the salt shaker is

3

not good enough.) Buy *liquid* dishwasher and washing machine soap. Clean up all spills immediately.

Because water evaporates so slowly in high humidity, it takes forever to get anything dry. Towels, swimsuits, floors, counters, even you, will be wet. It's a darn nuisance!

In all fairness, let me say that there are some benefits of a high humidity environment. Um ... let me see ... there must be something. Oh yes. The moisture "puffs up" clothes, skin and hair. This reduces the chore of ironing, makes for soft, smooth skin and if you happen to have wavy or curly hair, you'll have more – more waves, more curls, more hair! Contact lenses will be more comfortable (but the brilliant sunshine makes sunglasses mandatory). Well, yes, I am TRYING to be positive but it's difficult. Humidity is not a friend of mine.

I certainly have not won the war with this enemy. But I am well-equipped for battle and manage to hold my own now in the skirmishes on all fronts. As we go along, I will share my ammunition. This will help keep you out of the trenches.

SUMMER

July 1985

I was convinced I had contracted a fatal disease. Either that or some supernatural power was aging me a decade a day. Getting out of bed was a struggle; making breakfast required all the energy I had amassed through the night; I couldn't even vacuum more than one room at a time without resting; I was sticky. If I had a shower, in one hour I was sticky again. I couldn't wear my shoes, my feet had grown a size larger. I was near naked but contemplated ways to remove my skin. I had come from a place with 90 degree summers. I had never been so hot. It was summer in Bermuda. Five years would pass before I perfected a "vaccine" against this "disease". I'm still not immune to the symptoms, but they are no longer severe.

July 1990

I opened my eyes and looked to the right; the clock read 5 a.m. I looked to the left; the thermometer registered 83 degrees. It was going to be another one of those days – it was time to get moving.

This is one way to get your physical work completed in the hottest summer days – get up and get going EARLY in the morning. Being nocturnal myself, there are few things I dread more than early mornings, but hot afternoons are one of them. After many trials at reorganising my summer days, the early morning system has come out the clear winner. Rising early, to see the sun do the same, may be romantic, but for me, it's a case of self-preservation.

My problems with this season were compounded by my refusal to adjust my workload. I insisted on sticking to the same schedule as I kept in winter. To make matters worse, I am not a good vegetator. I cannot wistfully wile away the hours on the couch; I can't keep still that long. In the heat, I can't keep moving. If I can't keep still and I can't keep moving, what was I to do? The answer was a long time in coming. Accept what you cannot change. It is not possible to run around for sixteen hours in summer's heat. Change what you can. I implemented two systems: work an hour, rest an hour; and a complete reorganisation of my goals for the year. All physical work takes place in the winter; all sitting or thinking or creative-type work is left for summer.

It's still difficult for me to comprehend how a mere ten-degree rise in temperature can take me from comfort to exhaustion. Humidity, of course, plays a vital part in this. The human body, the miracle machine, has the answers to this. Heat opens the pores, expanding the surface of the skin to cooling. There is also a back-up system: perspiration. Fortunately, my skin does the expansion trick – so well that my dress and shoe size increase by one. Unfortunately, this is not the case, for me, when it comes to perspiration. Until I moved to Bermuda, I thought this was great – I never wore deodorant – didn't need to. Bathing was something I was supposed to do, not something I ever felt I needed. My first summer I was introduced to the feeling of "sticky". Not sweaty – sticky. As the years went by, I noticed a slight move towards adaptation. (Another dozen summers down the road, I should be able to boast that I too, sweat.) I relate this indelicate account to point out that we are all different. You probably have an excellent cooling system. But, just in case you don't, I have found an excellent substitute you might like to try. Fill an old spray bottle with water and spray yourself liberally throughout the day. If you don't have it (perspiration), create it.

That's not the end of it. You must be aware of the combined effect of temperature and humidity. A temperature of 85 at 90% humidity registers an apparent temperature of 102. In this range, prolonged exposure and physical activity can create sunstroke, heat cramps and heat exhaustion. An apparent temperature over 105 makes these results likely. I shudder everytime I see runners panting their way down South Road in July and August. (Newspaper article: *The Royal Gazette*, August 25, 1992 – Girl dies after training run: IRVINE, Calif. – An 18-year-old Cal-Irvine soccer player died three days after suffering heatstroke during a training run in 93-degree heat. Terrie Cate collapsed on Wednesday during a six-mile run. She died at Irvine Medical Centre on Saturday. Cate was the second student athlete to die during the heat wave that gripped Southern California last week. Sergio Echevarria, 17, suffered hypothermia and collapsed during football practice on Tuesday at San Fernando High. He died on Thursday. – AP.)

I deal with this temperature and humidity situation with the 150 system. If the total of the day's temperature and humidity, added together, equals or exceeds 150, I do not do any physically challenging work that day, i.e., temperature 85 degrees and humidity 75% added together equals 160, too high for hard work. This is a good time to write letters, read a book, go to the beach, be a tourist or go shopping. Most afternoons July through September will be over 150. If you have outside work to do, do it early or after 8 p.m. This is also a good time to sit outside in the cool of the evening; the stars seem close enough to touch. Plan to have your shower at midday when it will refresh you the most, have a nap in the afternoon, it's too hot to do anything else. If you have a nap, you'll also be all set to do more than sit after 9 p.m. when the house begins to cool down again.

Air conditioning is the answer to most of summer's problems. When we arrived here, only the most expensive homes boasted air conditioning. Now it is more the norm. If your new residence is not outfitted with this comfort, the second best solution is fans. Most homes have these, in one form or another, in several rooms. If the home you move into doesn't, you MUST get them. Ceiling fans are best as they are both efficient and out-of-the-way. The bigger the better and preferably the five-blade type. A medium setting will generally do the trick; on high, you will need a dozen paperweights to hold everything else down. One free source of air movement is Bermuda's breezes. Make the most of these by keeping your windows open, especially the ones opposite each other to create a good cross-draft.

One day, but probably not in my lifetime, man will turn to nature, the ultimate problem solver. For years I thought harnessing the power of the sun, wind and tides would not only create an energy efficient Bermuda, but would put into use these abundant, continuous resources. What a model for the world! Well ... to get back to reality ... eventually, a knowledgeable acquaintance pointed out to me that the power company did a major study on "my" energy solutions. As it turns out, we simply don't have enough land. Over a quarter of the island would be covered with wind turbines or solar panels. Conversion of the ocean's energy is cost-prohibitive. However, research is continuing with the Bermuda Electric Light Company investigating wind turbining at sea.

Water, remember water. Drink it, get into it, save it. A friend of mine has never been a "drinker" of anything. Although she is forty-five years old, she didn't have a problem until she hit a Bermuda summer. Then, kidney problems began. Her doctor explained that she needed additional quantities of water, or liquids of some kind, in this climate. She drank diligently. The problem went away. But then, she went back to her old low-fluid habit and, just like clockwork, the kidney problems flared up again. She now keeps a glass of water on the counter she walks by the most in a day. Each time she passes she takes a swig. This works for her. As I have some sort of liquid in my hands at all times, I don't have this problem, but be forewarned by this story. Summer or not, Bermuda or not, eight glasses of water a day is a healthy plan for us all. Because tap water here is not cold, keep a large jug of it in the fridge.

Iced tea is a popular summer drink. Making your own is easy. Put one-quarter cup sugar and one-quarter cup water in a glass measuring cup and microwave about two minutes until the sugar is dissolved. Add six cups of strong tea and two tablespoons lemon juice. Serve over ice. Lemonade is also a good choice. Make your own. Put one-quarter cup sugar and one-quarter cup water in a glass measuring cup and microwave for two minutes until the sugar is dissolved. Add one-half cup lemon juice and three cups of water. Serve over ice.

Summer time is drought time. So, do not be tempted to water your lawns and plants with the hose. If it's very dry, save your dishwater and bath water and use them. If you run just a couple of inches of water into the tub in the morning, you can jump in and out of it to cool yourself all day, then use it for your plants. If you shower, put a bucket in the tub with you. It will automatically catch a bucketful for later use.

At some point in our lives we learn a principle which, properly applied, will solve a thousand problems. We have these solutions stashed away in our brains. At times these surface from the depths. It was this way with talcum powder. After YEARS in Bermuda, it hit me. Wherever skin touches skin, use it – in the crooks of your elbows, behind the knees, under the breasts, on the inner thighs. It will stop these areas from sticking together and getting raw and sore. You can also use it in your shoes. Use it often and use it freely to stop these areas from sticking together.

Loose cotton clothing, preferably white, makes the summer wardrobe. If it's loose, the air will flow around it; if it's cotton, it will breathe and absorb perspiration. If it's white, the sun will keep it that way. Avoid elastics in tank tops or waistbands. Elastic anything will quickly create a wet perspiration line wherever it touches you. I thought my itsy, bitsy, teeny, weeny stretch tank tops would be ideal summer wear. I wore one once; I nearly suffocated. Shorts or culottes are great because they separate the skin of the upper inside thighs (something we do not naturally do, having been trained to keep our knees together!).

On the feet, too, less is more. For this season, forget high heels. Dressy summer occasions are often held outside. More than once, I spent an evening trying to stop my heels sinking into the ground. I'm told wedgies work well; a pair of flat dressy sandals will do fine. At this time of year your feet frequently become swollen and sore. Immersing hot, tired feet in a bucket of cool water brings immediate relief. I did the supper dishes this way for years! No, I don't do this anymore. I suppose that means I'm becoming a product of adaptation.

Find a way to keep your hair up. Mousse, gel, hairspray, ribbons, scarves, elastics, whatever works to keep the hair off the back of your neck will keep you cooler. Ideally, the shorter your hair the better for this season. Outside, wear a hat (preferably straw) and sunglasses. Moisture-laden air won't keep wrinkles at bay if you spend six months a year squinting in the bright sunlight!

I try to stay out of the sun this season. I do not want to cover myself in sunblock each day. Secondly, it seems one hour in the sun drains five hours from my energy stores. Normal day-to-day life supplies plenty of sunshine without seeking it out.

Summer is salad and barbecue time. Eat light – you won't be moving fast enough to burn off excess calories. Remember, even a five degree increase in temperature is noticeable – an oven is better left in the off position.

Buy *stone* coasters! These are fabulous because … they actually work! The drawback: they also stain. Be sure and keep the instructions for removing the inevitable coffee, tea and wine stains. If you don't want to buy the stone ones, remember, you will still need coasters AND cocktail napkins. Warm summer air in contact with a cold glass of liquid causes a mini flood. This is a real nuisance. Drops of condensed water will trail everywhere the glass goes, on the table, on your clothes, on you. I tried cork coasters. I tried sponge coasters. Both went mouldy. I washed them in sudsy water. This solution dissolved the glue and they fell apart. If you don't yet have the stone ones, stick with the tested and true – a cocktail napkin with a coaster. Yes, you will need both. The napkin will be soaked – the coaster stops the napkin from staining the furniture. A coaster alone simply provides a holding area for a puddle.

Your bedding also needs special attention at this time. These linens are absorbing perspiration all night. If you do not change them twice as often as usual, a strange odour will permeate your bedroom. I throw back the top sheet every morning and let the bed air for a few hours, preferably with the ceiling fan on. Every ten days or so, on a breezy day, I air the pillows and bedspread on the clothesline. (Do not do this if you plan to go out; it will surely rain!) A ten minute run in the dryer on the "fluff" setting works well too.

Use the sun and clothesline to keep your whites brilliant. On this note, try not to buy white clothing with coloured trim or decorations. While the whites will sparkle, the colours will fade. For the same reason, do not leave colours on the line for any length of time this season. To add some life to white outfits, try colourful jewellery, scarves or belts.

Of all the seasons, summer is my least favourite. I suppose you've figured that out for yourself by now. I am not alone. Some of the wealthier residents simply leave for the summer months. However, many of those I've spoken to disagree – especially those who work in air-conditioned offices AND Bermudians. On this note, let me say (just in case you are controlling the air conditioning in your office), PLEASE reduce it! Many, many employees spend the summer months freezing, in sweaters no less, because this cooling is taken to extreme. An office is quite comfortable at 75 degrees, especially when it's 85 outside. A ten degree differential is much less jarring to the human system when one is running in and out all day. In Bermuda, summer or winter, ten degrees will take you from discomfort to comfort. A temperature much below 75 is unnecessary, wasteful, costly and unhealthy.

Winter

It was March 1984. I was sitting in fetal position on a couch, fully dressed AND covered by my housecoat AND two blankets. My teeth were chattering. I wanted to climb into the closet that contained the hot water heater. I wanted to get into the car – it had a heater. I had come from a climate with 40 below zero winters; it was 50 degrees ABOVE zero this day. I had never been so cold. It was winter in Bermuda.

Winter ... I LOVE it! It never drops to 40 below. I do not have to spend fifteen minutes getting dressed like an Inuit to go outside. I can, though, wear clothes (yes!) on every part of my body, all day, all night! I can wear navy, black and burgundy again. I can even wear nylons and high heels AND my shoes fit! No ice, no snow and, most importantly, fewer bugs. I'm not blinded by sun at 6 a.m. and it actually gets dark BEFORE bedtime. Some days, the sun is not visible at all! I only have ONE shower a day! I can work – hard – ALL day. I can cuddle with my hubby on the couch under an afghan. It's just plain wonderful; if it were winter year round, I'd be one happy cowgirl.

But ... of course ... nothing's perfect. Anything below 60 degrees, in Bermuda, is uncomfortable. The record, set in February 1950, was 44. Generally, winter supplies about ten days of really cold (in the 50's) temperatures. That's not COLD, you may say. Yes ... well ... take my word for it; you'll be COLD. How, on earth, can that be true? There are two reasons for this. First, (take a guess) it's the humidity. If you are cold and wet, you'll be colder. If it's a high humidity day, the sweater you are wearing will be damp. Secondly, Bermuda homes do not contain furnaces – outside is inside, you don't escape it. I don't have a problem with this. Once I learned how to dress and how to keep the house dry, I had this one licked.

Layered, natural fibre clothing is the answer. On the top, I wear a cotton T-shirt, a cotton polo shirt (must have a collar) plus a sweater or sweatshirt. Warm slacks or track pants with tights or nylons, socks WITH slippers complete the outfit. (I have been planning to buy some long underwear for eight years now, but, because I haven't gotten around to it, I suppose it hasn't been that important. If you have some, bring them with you.) This is a warm, functional outfit for around the house. You cannot work in bulky coats or jackets. If you go outside, you'll be fine in this outfit as well (outside is inside). Think of how the body works. Cold hands, warm heart. If there is a perceived danger of chilling, the body sends more blood to the heart, to protect its most vital organ. This results in a lack of blood in the extremities. If your feet or hands are cold, warm your heart. This is the reason for triplicate layers on your chest. I see many blue-collar workers wearing toques in the winter. This is a sensible plan as a major loss of body heat takes place through the head. I haven't gotten into that practice though; I have thick hair which serves the same purpose. I also see toques in the summer. Haven't a clue what that's all about!

I keep a couple of afghans on the couch for rest times when I'm not moving enough to keep warm. For the bed, an electric blanket is mandatory. Not only will it warm the bed, but it will remove the dampness which has settled in through the day. Several news reports have stated that it's not wise to sleep in the electromagnetic field emitted by these blankets. You don't need to keep it on all night, simply preheat the bed before you retire and unplug the blanket before you climb in.

To warm the air you may want to try the following suggestions. Open all your windows, but not until 11 a.m. when the sun has warmed the air and dried the dew. Keep them open till 4 p.m. when you will notice a decided drop in temperature. This not only allows the warmed air in, but the breezes have a drying effect. This is important. You must not hibernate in a closed house all winter! It will be mouldy, smelly and wet. Get those windows open! If you have ceiling fans, most are equipped with a reverse button to push the warm air on the ceiling down (warm air rises). You may want to try this but I didn't find it particularly effective. Without a furnace generating heat, I surmise there IS no warm air to rise OR push down.

If you have air conditioning, you may also have heat as some models are equipped for this double duty. If you plan to install A/C in some form, consider this option.

Heaters of all sorts are available at the hardware stores. We tried a radiant type which shot up the power bill; we tried the space heater which couldn't cope with the open plan of the house. After we painted our fireplace, we gave up on fires too. As the answers to all questions are found in nature, I watched the animals. They know how to escape and survive every calamity. They all wanted to be in my closet! They cried at the door until I let them in. Of course! The closet is heated! Not only that but mine is a walk-in type! I set up a small table in there and spent many a cold evening typing letters home. I'm sure you can imagine the abundance of jokes from my family relating to Tracey's "sanctuary".

Tiled floors are very cold in winter. I use straw mats as scatter rugs. They're natural, a good colour, cheap, easily replaceable and can be cut to fit any area.

It's dark by five o'clock in the winter. So it's a good idea to have (just like home) a winter project. It's also best to keep moving. A brisk nightly walk will not only warm you up, but will improve your sleep, cardiovascular system and provide an excellent opportunity for some quality time with your hubby. Paul and I have planned the next forty years of our lives on our walks! This is also a good time to "Spring" clean, entertain and try all those hearty soup and stew recipes you have collected – anything that requires labour or heat. Stores and restaurants and hotels are warm, go there. Yes, you can wear your skimpy black dress out to dinner, elegant establishments are well heated.

Much of the rain in summer falls after midnight; it's not noticeable. Winter brings more rainy days – not lots, just more. Don't knock this; it's your water supply. But, if you are going out for several hours, it is important to close your windows. The rains can come in an instant and flood the streets in low lying areas. Imagine the mess it can make on the dresser under the window, the curtains and the carpet. If your transportation is a moped, you will need rain gear. This consists of a pair of rubber or vinyl pants and hooded jacket large enough to go over your everyday winter clothes. Rubber gumboots or overshoes and warm, waterproof gloves will complete this outfit. Many riders wear a scarf on the coldest days. This outfit should be carried with you all winter. To complete your kit, add a brown paper grocery bag. Placing the bag over your chest and under your coat provides amazingly effective insulation against winter's biting winds.

I think of winter as December to April. December can be chilly, but we've spent many sunny, 75-degree Christmas Days walking along the beach. January is the month of winds; gales are common. Take in your lawn furniture and umbrella. The first three months of the year are the coldest. You may find this period takes a long time to pass. For me, it's simply not long enough.

SPRING & FALL

Spring is the month of May. Fall is November. May should be your busiest month. Preparation is key.

May is the final month for summer preparations. This is the time to complete any major cleaning; you will not have the stamina to wash walls in August! In November you can pick it up again and you'll be set for Christmas. That's all you need to remember about November. Back to May.

Make a point of using up as much cupboard food as possible and put the rest in the fridge. This will avoid ants in the cereal, weevils in the pasta and soggy crackers. Only keep on hand what you will consume soon; do not stock the freezer. Power failures from hurricanes can last for days. Start thinking iced tea, lemonade, salad and BBQ; dig out those great summer recipes to try.

Wash and retire the afghans, slippers, blankets – anything not made of cotton. Dig out your lightweight, light-coloured cottons and get them ironed. Clean the spider webs out of your white shoes and purses. All dark clothing should be cleaned, turned inside-out and covered or kept in a dark place, away from sunlight. Wrap dark purses and shoes in tissue paper. This sounds like a lot of hassle, but it will pay off – your shoes will not be mouldy and your clothes will not be faded.

Torture ... is nylon stockings in August! Can't be done. Prepare for this eventuality in May also. The weather is perfect for a daily ten minute session in the sun. Tan those legs and forget nylons till November. And, forget nylon panties too.

Dig out your swimsuit and check the fit. Check your towels and earmark those in the worst shape for beach towels. Buy some suntan lotion. Choose six books and videos to entertain you in the days it will be too hot to do anything else. Summer is a time for quiet pursuits. Write a book! Okay ... a letter.

As much as I love winter, these two months, May and November are my favourites. The temperature is about 75 – very pleasant, no extremes. Evening temperatures drop 10 degrees from the daily high. That's fine in May and November, 65 is still in the comfort zone. Everything considered, Spring and Fall in Bermuda are just about perfect.

EMILY

It was 7 a.m. I was asleep. Somewhere in the fog I heard voices. Paul was speaking to our son, Scott. I heard – at least I thought I heard, "You won't be going to school today." This could ONLY mean, the Second Coming was upon us.

It wasn't. But, there was an arrival. As the T-shirts (which came later) read, "The bitch came to breakfast."

This was the unforgettable morning of Hurricane Emily. There wasn't time to be afraid. She snuck up in the middle of the night; everyone was asleep when the warnings were issued. In one hour, she had come and gone leaving us with the scenery of a war zone.

I had, of course, researched hurricanes. Not since 1906 had anyone been killed in a Bermuda hurricane. Emily's havoc did not break that record. You couldn't be safer than in Bermuda. Homes made of stone and concrete blocks are not going anywhere! Even my dozen chickens, left to fend for themselves, survived without injury. The worst part came three days later.

The first day was ... interesting, challenging. By the third day we were downright miserable. We had honeymooners in the bed and breakfast room; we had guests in the cottage. They were not having fun. Neither were we. The fridge and freezer food had to go; we were desperately in need of a shower; everything was wet and smelly. We had spent the first two evenings catching up on our correspondence, writing by candlelight. We'd run out of friends to write to. We were no longer in control of our environment and it was most distressing to realize, with total clarity, just how dependent we were on the energy source called electricity. In our case, we "did without" for five days.

In others, three weeks. Some sensible residents simply got a plane and got out of here – to a place with power.

Every cloud has a silver lining and this was the case with Emily. Many power poles, long past their prime, came down; old, diseased and weak trees did the same. Nature cleaned house. The Emergency Measures Organisation moved into full gear to upgrade their systems. We all had a lesson in preparation and response. Batteries, candles and tarpaulins became a mandatory part of summer supplies.

It's not likely we will again experience a power loss the duration of Emily's. Nor is it likely we will have so little warning. But, just in case, preparation is key.

I start thinking about hurricanes in August. Until then, the ocean has not warmed enough to sustain these swirling winds. Your senses will tell you when conditions are ripe. You will be hot, sticky and weary from many days of hot, humid weather. A swim in the ocean will feel like a bath. You will think you simply cannot take one more day of beautiful Bermuda sunshine. As the storm approaches, the ocean gets angry. The South Shore becomes a lion, roaring displeasure. The waves increase, picking up swirling sand, changing the crystal blue water to an opaque green. Two layers of clouds are visible in the sky – two different types – moving in opposite directions. The animals get nervous. The birds disappear. Winds increase and rain begins.

For the uninitiated, I recommend you begin preparing when you first hear the word "hurricane" mentioned. This will be early June, the start of hurricane season. Get yourself a cup of coffee and the phone book. Yes, the phone book. This is the first Bermuda book you should browse through. Go to the blue pages. Here you will find all sorts of interesting, pertinent information as well as a clear, concise guide of what to do before, during and after these and less violent storms. While *Tea With Tracey* may be lost in a closet somewhere, the telephone book is always readily accessible and easy to find. Read this information in June and read it again when the first warnings are issued or when your senses tell you "something is up".

If this subject causes you distress, try to think of it as … an adventure … a new experience … an exciting subject for your next letter home. It is certainly not a boring time! You can even have fun with it. Several businesses offer hurricane-tracking maps. Get one and chart the storm as it approaches. Pay attention to the clues in the environment. See if you can spot them. Accept that you are one with nature

– part of it – because you are. Take the necessary precautions, follow the guide and, then, relax. There is nothing more you can do.

First and foremost, do not panic. You are going to survive this. You will probably get all your mail answered as well!

Just before I leave this subject, let me mention a related phenomenon before someone else does and scares you to death. I hesitate to use the word "earthquake" ... minor tremor is a better description. I'm only aware of two. I slept through the first one, but it woke Paul and our daughter, Cassy. There was some talk that it may have cracked a few water tanks – I didn't hear much more about it. For the second one, I was awake. I felt a "shimmy" in the arm I had resting on the table. And that was the end of it. On your list of things to worry about, rate this one a zero.

CHAPTER TWO

The Enemy Within

STORAGE

We arrived on the island on July 4. I was advised to bring everything we owned as goods were expensive here. I could sell whatever I didn't need for more than I could in Canada. As well as eight suitcases, "everything" amounted to a full container. It took me four months just to sort and settle the NECESSITIES into their respective places. All the rest went into an empty bedroom and remained there until the Christmas festivities ended and our first set of guests returned home. When I finally tackled the storage bedroom, I had an instant replay of "Tough Morning". But, this was worse. How could it be? It went on for a week!

My navy, burgundy and black clothes were polka-dotted with some sort of grey powder, my brown leather goods were green, the furniture had turned grey. My old books were in pieces, corners were missing, the pages were damp, wrinkled, smelly and spotted. The matting on my pictures was in this same state, but the oil paintings were not – they were warped. Anything made of metal was rusted or pitted or corroded. The hanging devices on my decorative plates had come unglued. This entire scene of neglect was interlaced with cobwebs and creatures of all sorts – both living and dead. I was not impressed. The moral of this story: use it or lose it.

You must keep things moving. You must keep them clean, and you must allow them sun and light and air. Keep only what you are prepared to use – AND CLEAN – on a regular basis. Get rid of the rest, as soon as possible. You cannot have a house like Grandma's with goods stored since World War II. Contrary to the advice I was given: if you don't REALLY need it, DON'T bring it with you. This culling process requires deep thought. Actually, there is very little you REALLY need. Half of what you presently own is useless here. Half of what you do need, you don't yet own!

Leave your leather at home. It's the dickens to look after in this climate. The same goes for books. They're available, second-hand, for under a dollar. Do not bring boxes of envelopes or greeting cards. They self-seal in the humidity. If well-meaning friends or relatives present you with a box of stationery, nip this problem in the bud. by inserting a small piece of wax paper between the back of the envelope and the flap. It's a pain, but it works. A closed envelope can also be ironed open (and everyone asks, "What do you DO here?"). These are but two of the 456 unique chores that may now fill your time too.

Number 301 is sprinkling talcum powder in anything made of rubber (swim caps, gloves etc.). They have a tendency to melt together. Remember the vinyl jackets so popular in the late '80's? Mine met this fate. Tissue paper also prevents this. Insert it between the places rubber touches rubber. Or, how about this one? Putting one-third of a wine cork behind your hanging pictures? This allows air circulation between the picture and the wall. Yes, walls are damp. At this point, I might mention a great way to get a free ticket home: write a letter to your family explaining that you have spent the day cutting wine corks into thirds! Or ironing envelopes!

Okay now, I'm getting off track. I didn't finish the "falling plate" story. We awoke to a crash in the night. Inspection showed one of our wall-mounted collector's plates in pieces on the floor. The other three fell a week later. As well as glueing things together (envelopes), humidity "unglues" them (hangers on the back of plates). This is also the case with those beautiful little crystal ornaments. The ears fell off my rabbit, the eyes fell off my turtle and the rooster lost his tail. These can be repaired with epoxy glue, which I've done ... twice. Even this heavy duty, super duper bonding miracle lives a short life in Bermuda.

Now, on to clothing. Before storing, items of any composition must be CLEAN. Invisible material (perspiration, fingerprints) will serve as food for mildew or bugs. Even cleaning will not ensure against this, but it's your best defense. There's a term used here: "closet spots". These are small yellow dots that just appear on some types of stored clothing. Depending on the fabric and colour of the garment, bleach, sunlight, hot, soapy water and/or dry cleaning fluid may remove the worst of it. Often, there's no hope. Even if you meet with success, the same article, stored again, ends up in the same state. Get rid of these problem articles after the first go-round or keep them in constant use.

A bright or sun-filled closet is a great defense against mildew, but ... every silver lining has a cloud. Even a light bulb in constant use will fade fabric. To prevent this, dark clothes should be turned inside out and covered with something like a white cotton bed sheet. Clothing should not be left in the plastic drycleaner bags – use only fabric or paper coverings. On a sunny, breezy day, clean your closet and air your stored clothes on the clothesline for a few hours.

This brings us to the subject of closet heaters. You MUST have them. Generally, these are long, rod-shaped tubes of metal that supply enough extra heat to hold the moisture in the air (the warmer the air, the more moisture it can hold). If the moisture is in the air, it's not in your clothes. In a small closet, a constantly burning light bulb will do the trick as well. Spores are constantly in the air. Not much can be done about that. But, moving air prevents them from settling and multiplying. On low humidity days, I open all windows and doors, closets and cupboards, to allow this moving, dry air free reign. A fan, of any type, gives the same results. You will certainly need a heater. Step into your closet, close the door, take a whiff. If, despite the heater, you still smell mould, get a fan, get a bigger heater or get a heater with a fan.

Don't wait to see if these problems are going to happen. They will. Get on to this as soon as you arrive. Save yourself the grief. Forewarned is forearmed. I wasn't. You are.

MILDEW

We had been in Bermuda long enough for me to have searched out, found and replaced all our curtains. Even though they were new, I still wasn't happy. They hung at the windows limp and lifeless. One morning, as I sat nursing my coffee and pondering this, the answer emerged from the depths. Starch! Of course! Down came the curtains. I washed them, starched them, ironed them and put them back up. They looked great! Crisp! New! I had to admit, I was one smart cookie. Well ... not exactly. Two weeks later, they looked disgusting. Far from being lifeless, they were now a support system. No one had told me: starch is a food source for moulds. HOW was I supposed to know all this stuff? Good grief.

Technically, mould and mildew are not the same. However, I use the two words interchangeably (so does everyone else I know). One reason for this: the words "mildewy" (if there is such a word) or "mildewed" sound like marbles in the mouth. For our purposes here, it doesn't make any difference. For the scientists among you, please excuse this lack of accuracy. I'm trying hard NOT to be too technical.

As well as fabrics, other materials are prone to mildew attack: painted items, Tupperware and dark furniture, for example. What we are discussing here is a living organism – with a very weird diet! It is not necessarily feeding on the paint or plastic, but rather on the thin film of dust and invisible organic material that accumulates on these surfaces. (Keep it clean!) Painting a mouldy surface is a useless exercise.

Unlike most other living organisms, moulds need no oxygen to survive. They will grow right through the new layer of paint. If you plan to spruce up that little apartment you've just moved into, do not paint until you have removed the mould. It is much easier to wash a wall than paint it. Chances are good that once it's washed, it won't need paint. Bleach kills mould. Soap removes dirt. To kill the mould and clean the surface, wash with a solution of one tablespoon dry laundry detergent and one quart of bleach to three quarts warm water. Then, rinse with water. When we paint these days, we buy mildew-resistant paint or have the paint clerk add a bottle of mildewcide at the store.

While we're discussing paint and bleach ... one thing bleach will NOT do is keep white paint white. It's the weirdest thing. Twice we painted the kitchens and bathrooms white in both the house and cottage. Within a year, everything was off-white. The sun must do this which is also quite strange as it TAKES the colour from everything else! If you do any white or off-white painting here, you might as well ask for a colour called moonstone as this is what it will end up as anyway. The sun also removes yellow from colours quite quickly so your green will become blue and so on.

Oops, sorry, I kind of got off-track there. I know you just can't wait to get back to mildew.

In my quest for the solutions to this endless problem, I tried everything. Mildew inhibitors got a lot of attention. These packets of chemicals (paradichlorobenzene and paraformaldehyde) emit vapours that inhibit mildew growth. In tightly enclosed areas they do this job well, but the smell from these vapours is enough to kill a horse! They are poisonous, they damage some plastics and they must be replaced as soon as the smell disappears. This was just too complicated for me.

Bleach is your best buddy in the battle for control of mildew. In addition to walls, it can be used on furniture, plastics, porcelain, stainless steel, tile – all sorts of things. But, and this is important, read the bleach bottle instructions! And, this too is important, read the soap box or container of any other product you plan to mix with bleach. So many soaps these days have additives that will create noxious gases and poisons if mixed with bleach. Be careful with this. Read the instructions! I haven't seen any instructions on bleach bottles for bleaching furniture so I'll give you the ratio I use: one gallon of water to half a cup of bleach. Immediately remove this solution with a dry cloth. This will kill the mould, but it will return. All bleaching is but a temporary cure, so again, work on prevention. As I've said before and will say ten times more: keep it clean, keep it moving and keep it dry.

Please keep in mind that bleach is tough on the environment. Whenever, wherever possible, use the same bleach mixture for as many jobs as you can. Mix your solution in a container that needs cleaning (maybe your dishpan?), add your dish cloth and tea towel and use these to clean your cupboard, wall, sink, tub and finally, the toilet or kitty litter. In this way, one cup of bleach goes a long way both financially and environmentally. Also, choose one set of clothes as your bleaching outfit and put that on BEFORE you open the bleach bottle. I have a whole wardrobe of bleaching clothes now because: this would just take a minute, I just needed a little bit, it was just one spot, I'd be careful, etc. Yes. Well. If you have an old white housecoat, press it into service for this chore.

What DO I do here? Well ... I spend a lot of time thinking AND remembering AND researching AND questioning. It's important to stop and think. Try your best to remember your high school science classes. Physics (warm air holds moisture), chemistry (moisture and oxygen produce rust), and biology (chlorine kills mould) principles provide many clues to the solutions of a multitude of dilemmas. My son, Scott, a science major, was quite anxious to get off to university to escape my daily barrage of questions. Well ... I NEED to know these things. This isn't a personality trait Bermuda has created. As a child, I recall my mother saying (more than once), "Tracey, if I had answers to all your questions, I'd be in the Pentagon." This, of course, was no help to me at all. It begged the inevitable question, "What's the Pentagon?" Guess I missed my calling. I should have been a scientist.

APPLIANCES

It was above my eye level. I hadn't yet learned that keeping house in Bermuda involved standing on chairs and kneeling on floors. This ritual was one of discovery. Strange things were happening in out-of-the-way places.

Little brown specks covered the top of the fridge. With a sinking feeling, I realized ... this was rust. Good grief! This appliance was only six months old! How was it going to last twenty years? Yep, it was time again to stop ... and think.

Aha! I had an idea. A piece of newspaper would catch the dust, absorb any moisture and keep the top clean. It wouldn't be noticeable and I could change it often, at no cost. Bingo! Well, not quite. The cat also thought this was a dandy idea. The newspaper became her new bed. I was left with *The Royal Gazette* printed all over the top of the fridge.

I then replaced the newspaper with a tablecloth. Surely, that was the answer. It wasn't. The cloth did absorb the moisture but it never seemed to dry: wet cloth, laying on metal, no, this was not a good plan.

I moved to plan C. After intensive research, I found the recommended way to protect appliances: new, blue, poly car wax. Reputed to be the best thing since sliced bread, and recommended by appliance manufacturers, this would do it. It protected cars by forming a shield, impenetrable to the elements. Sounded good to me. I applied three coats. I guess I had waited too long; the rust had begun and it continued to spread. I bought appliance touch-up paint and applied it with a nail polish brush. That lasted six months. I gave up.

The next fridge we bought was a "tropicalised" model made especially for climates with high humidity. The exterior is covered with a type of vinyl coat which should be impervious to rust. However, my appliance repairman confirms that the rust is initiated INSIDE and I now have rust coming through the vinyl. Is there no end to this?

My washer and dryer are located at the back door entrance; they are subject to use as a counter. They serve as a temporary resting spot for helmets, bike bags, tools, purses and anything else coming in the back door. They had to have some protection. After the waxing procedure, I covered them with a quilted cotton pad. These two appliances were purchased the same time as the fridge but are in much better shape. This could be a result of the window three feet away, the heat from the dryer, the pad or simply a better finish coat from the factory. I haven't figured it out yet.

My original oven was built ... oh ... about 50 BC. I never did have to clean it; I just swept out the rust each week. Now that I have a replacement, I take care to wipe off all the horizontal surfaces as a part of my daily kitchen tidy up. The installer of the new oven explained that these "newfangled" models are only built to last eight years so I guess that's a solution in itself. Boy, is this planet going to be a mess – an appliance junkyard.

If you purchase new appliances here, this is what I recommend you do. Immediately apply the wax, three coats. (Logically, it must help.) Then, keep it CLEAN. When moisture, dust and salt from the air settles, it begins the rust process. If the appliances you have are too far gone for these suggestions, you could check into having them professionally repainted.

Rust is inevitable. In preparation for this eventuality, I suggest you keep two products on hand: WD 40™ and Pam™. Both are oils in spray cans. To loosen rusted parts or clean metal, WD 40™ works great. It also provides pro-active protection for boat engines, tools and garden equipment. Pam™, an edible product, protects your barbecue from the elements. Once it's *cool* and clean, give it a spray.

PARTS

I could tell you a story of epic proportions about the microwave. I could tell you the saga of the computer. I could tell you about the frying pan, the kettle, the iron, the coffee maker and the toaster. Each one of these broke down. Each one of them set us off on a mission impossible: to find the parts and a repairman to fix them. We gave up on the microwave mission after a year and a half. We stuck with the computer saga for several years. When we were told the parts were not available, we ordered them ourselves. We paid amounts (called *deposits*) to repairmen – the STILL-BROKEN items were returned but NOT the deposits. We made dozens of telephone calls, wrote letters, delivered parts ourselves. We tried everything, but, in the end, we had to admit defeat. Although both Paul and I strongly believe in the principle of reuse, recycle, repair, we had to question whether it was worth the time, the aggravation, the energy, the money.

Bermuda is not unique in this regard. We now live in a disposable world and we know this. However, we do try to do our bit for the good of this planet and the pocketbook! Technology, the invention of plastic and mass production have made it next to impossible to repair any item for less than the cost of a new one – so much for the pocketbook. I must assume, for this same reason, that parts and the small appliance repairman have met the same fate as the dinosaur. Being on an island, with a small population, intensifies the problem.

At first, I thought all these breakdowns must have had something to do with the electrical supply. Two electricians checked our house and found nothing amiss. Then, I thought it had something to do with the electric company itself. I couldn't justify this charge, though, as some of the appliances, especially the larger ones, were doing fine. We installed surge protectors on our big-ticket items and unplugged everything when a storm approached. I also mused over the possibility that small pieces inside these electrical items may have been made of iron or steel. Given this climate, they were bound to rust. This is a possibility. Whatever, we have given up trying to locate the reason. Now, knowing that a short life span is inevitable, we purchase only the most reasonably priced, no frill models. When they give up the ghost, out they go.

Bring or buy only what you use on a regular basis. You've heard this before. It's especially important in the case of small appliances. If you are accustomed to a gourmet kitchen, this may be difficult but it will save you much grief. If your contract is a short one, there is just no point in exposing all your carefully collected gadgets to ruin for the sake of a couple of uses while you're here. And, unless your hubby is very handy and travels abroad often enough to pick up parts, it's not worth the aggravation. Just last week, in the middle of mixing up an angel food cake, my Mixmaster™ caught on fire. After dealing with that, I grabbed the Dustbuster® to pick up a few crumbs on the floor and it no longer worked. I don't agonize over these things anymore. Accept what you cannot change.

POLISHING

"So," I asked my crew of three, "if you found out, beyond a doubt, that I was an Iraqi spy, would you turn me in?"

I thought it was kind of neat at first. All four of us sitting, on an old sheet, on the living room floor, chatting, working together to complete the task at hand. I would pick a controversial topic like ... capital punishment, abortion, euthanasia or the one above. This would get the adrenalin going and spur us on. It took two Sundays to finish the job but it was worth it. We admired our work as we went from room to room – for a month. Then, depression set in. We had to start again! It took four people, two Sundays to complete a job that lasted four Sundays. (What's wrong with this picture?) Something had to change. The job was polishing brass. The change? We got rid of it.

It took some time to come to this decision. I had determined the perfect spot for each piece and we all loved the look of sunshine settling on the rich golden metal. We would also have to replace all these ornamental and functioning pieces with something else. Before we reached this drastic decision, I did my research (yes, again). We tried three types of polish; we looked into having everything lacquered, we did the new, blue, poly wax trick. We bundled it all up and took it to the workshop at St. Brendan's Hospital. But, in the end, the pain outweighed the pleasure. We simply had more brass than one family could handle. Ten percent of the time it looked fabulous; ninety percent of the time it looked disgraceful. I do not recommend bringing your brass or copper or silver collection here. You just don't need the hassle. If you buy brass fans, buy the ones with the antique brass finish. That's how they'll look anyway, once rust, pitting and corrosion sets in.

While we're on the subject of metals, wire coat hangers rust. Trade them in for ones made of wood or plastic. Pins, needles, staples, paper clips, scissors and tweezers meet the same fate. Wherever possible, bring only those items made of stainless steel or aluminum – not iron or steel. (Even aluminum will corrode but this takes a long time.) Buy plastic-covered paper clips. Keep small metal objects in a closed container, add a piece of chalk or two. Chalk absorbs moisture. Put a few pieces in the tool box. While you're at it, put a few pieces in a hat or shoe or scarf box – no moisture, no rust (or mould).

Here again, remember chemistry class. Know your enemy. Rust is a product of oxidation. When iron or steel is exposed to damp air, the process begins. Three elements are necessary: iron or steel, air and moisture. Remove any one of these and the problem is solved. Don't buy anything made of iron or steel; keep the ones you have out of the air; keep the moisture away. A messy but effective protector for tools is a coating of grease or oil. Moisture and air can't penetrate this. Along this line, I used Vaseline to coat many small articles – latches, closures, screws and nails. I didn't get rust, but it was just not practical, too messy. Keep this is mind though, you may have a situation where it will work for you.

WATER

There's a pineapple in the pipe!

The system is so simple, it's scary. Rain is collected from the roof, stored in a tank under the house and pumped up when needed. With all the fuss over drinking water and chemicals the last twenty years, I was leery about this untreated liquid, not to mention the cleanliness of the roof and the exact contents of the tank. For all I knew, someone could have died down there! I called in the professionals.

The Health Department took samples, tested and concluded that everything was normal and safe. Having obviously dealt with wary types such as myself, they did suggest, if I was still concerned, I could chlorinate the water. This is done by calculating the cubic feet of water in the tank and adding regular household bleach. To find the cubic feet, multiply the length times the width times the depth of water in the tank. Then, multiply this figure by 6.25 to find how many gallons. Then add 2 ounces of bleach for each 1000 imperial gallons. This we did. It was comforting to know that we had killed every living organism in there and that, for now, all was pure. However, I was not impressed with either the taste or smell and I have not repeated the procedure since.

I do not believe this is a necessary exercise. If you are concerned, have it checked. If you get very low on water, have the tank professionally cleaned. By law, a water tank should be cleaned every five years, but I don't know anyone who adheres to this. Bleach is not a solution to a dirty tank. Chemicals in the bleach react with the sludge collected at the bottom. A relatively clean tank will not produce problem reactions by the addition of bleach. But then, a clean tank shouldn't need bleach. Be sure your roof is painted regularly enough to keep it white. For us, this is every three years, but we can stretch it to four or five by having the roof scrubbed with a solution of 50% bleach and 50% water after the second year. This is about a third of the cost of painting. Be sure all the tank openings are screened and gutters are cleaned of accumulated debris. Prevent strange things getting into your tank with the use of "pineapples". These are small, plastic, cone-shaped devices which fit over gutter pipe openings and act as strainers. Check and see if they are on those openings. If not, buy some and put them on.

An average water tank holds 20,000 gallons but many are much smaller or shared by several families. At some point, you may need to buy water. This is simply a matter of calling a supplier. He will deliver 800 – 1,000 gallon truckloads and pump it into your tank. However, keep in mind, if you are low, many others are too. The waiting list for delivery could stretch to two weeks. Check your tank periodically, especially when those around you are talking of water shortages. Order BEFORE you're in a crisis. Two weeks without water is a *nightmare*. The Health Department suggests bleaching purchased water, boiling the drinking water and asking the trucker the source of his supply. To bleach small quantities of water use one drop per liter or 4 drops per gallon.

To avoid the nuisance of buying water, do not be wasteful with this precious liquid. This is not difficult. Unless your tank is small, or cracked, all you need will be there. Note the word "need". You must explain this to any guests who arrive; they are often the cause of water problems. We are subject to near drought conditions from time to time; you will know when we are; everyone will be talking about it. Even if your tank is full now, conserve for these times. Use a dishpan in your sink, use bath water for plants, shower quickly and turn off the taps while you apply shampoo and creme rinse. Remind your hubby to turn off the tap while shaving and brushing teeth. Fix a leaky faucet immediately. Be sure the rain is actually going into your tank; we just fished out a *pineapple*, with accumulated debris. This had somehow become lodged in the downpipe creating a massive waterfall over the side of the house instead of into the tank. A tennis ball did the same thing. Keep your gutters clear of dead leaves, seeds and such for the same reason.

Be sensible. Be aware. Think. An early morning shower is not necessary if you'll be on the beach before noon.

Remember, Bermuda water is soft. It has always been my practice to wear rubber gloves when washing dishes. For this reason, I didn't realize how "slippery" my dishwater was until I broke a dozen dishes. If, up to now, you've worked with hard water, cut your soap additions by half – in the sink, in the washer, in the shower.

More tea? Bermuda water makes good tea, don't you think?

You know, when I first met Paul, back in my other life, I asked him to tell me about Bermuda. He said rain was the water supply. As I sat there, smiling sweetly and trying to look intelligent, I distinctly remember thinking, "You have got to be kidding!" In the same instant, I also made a decision: Paul's birthplace would never see the likes of this little cowgirl. Yes ... well ... what do I know?

ELECTRICITY

Rain is free, electricity is not. Here, too, you must conserve or pay the penalty. Air conditioning solves a multitude of problems. It cools the air (mould needs heat) and it lowers the humidity (rust and mould need moisture). It is also expensive; exercise control. Keeping the temperature at 75 degrees in summer is quite comfortable (I keep ours at 80). Don't leave lights, fans, the television or any appliance on if it's not serving a purpose. If you travel, unplug your hot water heater and anything else an empty house does not require. Many residents have installed timers on their water heaters and report substantial savings. These shut off the water heater in the late evening and turn it back on in the early morning. If this method alone saves money, imagine what savings can be had by exercising control in all areas! If your property contains an apartment or cottage, unplug all electrical appliances when it's vacant. This may all sound like common sense, but I am aware of the unbridled waste of both electricity and water every time I leave the island. Let your guests know that this is not acceptable.

Storms often cause a loss of power. When the damage is repaired and the power comes back on, a surge of electricity goes through the wires. This can cause the "death" of the appliance or, worse, an explosion. For this reason, unplug whatever you can in a storm and use surge protectors on your high-ticket items. This is purely a precaution, "death" and explosions are rare.

Keep your outside power lines free from plant growth. Trees entangled in these lines will, sooner or later, cause a power interruption. Prevention is key.

DEHUMIDIFIER

I think I'll go and work in the cottage, it's only 60% over there.

Two years after our arrival here, I was still trying to come to grips
with this humidity business. I had learned that while the term "humidity" referred to the amount of water vapour in the air, the term "relative humidity" was this amount compared to the amount the air could
hold at a given temperature. A 20 degree increase in temperature dou-
bled the air's capacity to hold moisture. This explained why closet
heaters worked; why it rained more in winter; why it rained more at
night. Learn one principle and away we go! I was feeling very intelligent but not moving forward. I needed more help. I needed some
"tools".

My son bought me a hygrometer. It read 60% for six years. My ever-
so-accommodating husband sought out a German model. I had complete faith in this little piece. We all know the German reputation for
quality. It registered 90% the day I received it and I thought, ALL
RIGHT, now we're cooking with gas! It measured 90% for the next
three years.Five years later, I discovered this hygrometer needed to be
properly calibrated. For this, I needed a Sling Psychrometer. Yeah,
right. Now where did I put my Sling Psychrometer? Sheesh. I set about
to find an alternate method. Bingo! This is done by wetting a piece of
cotton and wrapping it around the air holes, leaving the scale and
adjustment screw visible. After 30 minutes, with the cloth still in place,
turn the adjustment screw so that the scale reads 95%. Remove the
cloth, wait 30 minutes and the reading will then be accurate. Not that
you'll EVER need to know this. Sigh. I gave up on the tools.

By this time I had discovered that the weather station gave up-to-
date forecasts (including humidity) several times daily. I phoned them
every morning. It wasn't long before I could determine it myself with
the aid of my senses (see "Tough Morning"). Okay, now I had identified the problem, measured it and studied it; all that was left to do was
to reduce it and my problems, all fifty of them, would be over.

Research provided two solutions: an air conditioner or a dehumidifier. You've heard the air conditioner story. Plan B: We bought a
dehumidifier. We tried it in the house that summer. If the humidity
was making it so darn hot, the lowering of it would have to make it

cooler. The house got hotter. Hot air blew out the front of this machine. The windows had to be closed. This in itself drove me crazy. We lost the cooling effect of the breezes; we were cooped up; I couldn't hear the birds or the rustling of leaves; the world was too silent. (I am forever opening windows. When I go back to Canada now, this, plus my ranting about turning off lights and running taps, drives my hosts to drink!)

If you have a storage room, unused bedroom or empty guest apartment, a dehumidifier is a good investment. We use one in our guest cottage when it's vacant. This saves me the daily ritual of opening and closing windows which, in turn, keeps the dust down, the bugs out and the mould, mildew and rust at bay. It can keep the humidity at 60%. That's a whole lot better than 90.

If you decide to purchase one of these machines, a few precautions are in order. Dehumidifiers are not effective under 60 degrees – the coils freeze up, shutting down the motor. Be aware of this in winter and unplug it on the coldest days. Also, don't forget to empty it daily. Use this water for plants or gardens. The shut-off mechanism on our model didn't last long. Yes, floods. I had it fixed. It broke down again. It still won't shut off when full so I just make sure it's part of my daily routine: empty the dehumidifier – job 437. On very humid days, I empty it twice.

FURNITURE

Why is everything pink?

We brought everything with us. I do not recommend this. Leave the furniture at home. Are you beginning to realize how little you should bring?

First of all, you don't know for sure that you'll be staying. Even if you do, there's no guarantee that you will want to, or be able to, renew your permit. Two years is really just an extended holiday; it will be gone in a flash!

Secondly, moving furniture is an expensive business. Packaging, insurance, freight and duty charges must be paid – not to mention the stress of waiting and wondering.

Thirdly, if you have "good stuff", you are risking breakage; if you don't, why haul it around? Chances are, the insurance will not cover the repairs of those items broken in shipping. Then, of course, you must track down a professional to fix it, engage in the waiting game and hope you are satisfied with the results. Obviously, I've seen this movie.

Fourthly, the second-hand market in Bermuda is alive and well. The transient nature of the population and the high standard of living ensure a constant supply of items from leaving-island-sales, garage sales, auctions, consignment sales, and fundraising events. Not only can you find unique and antique items this way, but these pieces have completed their acclimatization. If they were subject to splitting, cracking, shrinking, swelling, rusting, fading or discoloration, it's already happened. What you see is what you get. I am still trying to effect repairs on dresser drawers that will not open. The wood absorbed the moisture in the air and expanded them enough to seal them shut. I've used candle wax, soap and sandpaper. Now I need to get a plane (not the one that flies, the tool!). Two coffee tables, with no room to expand, split down the middle. The varnish on four wood chairs "melted" into a sticky layer capable of catching everything floating in the air as well as the back of any sitter.

Fifthly (is there such a word?), it's quite possible that whichever home you rent or buy will be wholly or partially furnished already. Until you have settled in, you won't know exactly what you need. One thing you certainly do NOT need is twice as much furniture as you can possibly use.

Moreover, chances are, whatever you have is not pink. Everything in Bermuda is pink: houses, clothes, furniture, drapes, me …. Your black Oriental couch will attract mould; your dark brown furniture will do the same. So will navy and burgundy. It just isn't practical to decorate with these colours – the sun will fade them quickly and they look out of place here. Pastels and whites in a sunny room will save you a lot of heartache.

Remember the recommendation to leave leather clothes behind? The same goes for leather furniture. In summer, much skin is exposed. Skin, in contact with leather or plastic or rubber, in the heat, is most uncomfortable. You will have to peel yourself off these materials. Notice, I am sitting on a towel on the chair; my right arm is resting on a potholder on the table. Both the table and chair are covered with plastic. It's July.

If there are special pieces you must bring, ensure that they are packed as tightly as possible. Fill every inch of the container or crate. If even the smallest space is left for movement, rubbing, gouging and breakage will be the result.

Bermuda walls are concrete or stone. Keep this in mind when packing or purchasing pictures and mirrors. Placement requires more than hammer and nail. You will need a drill, wall plugs and fixtures, especially for the heavier hanging decorations. One more time: bring only, buy only, what you NEED.

WINDOWS

I was at it again. Thinking, that is. Something had to be done about the forty-eight feet of windows in the enclosed verandah. The previous owner had draped them in a blue, green and yellow lattice print. Although they were lined, only the bottom two feet showed any sign of this pattern. The lining had shredded; between the lining and pattern lay half a dozen dead roaches. All in all, they were quite a sight.

What in the world was I going to replace them with? A pattern or color would meet the same fate. Even lining hadn't prevented this. They would have to be white. Oh Lord, what a state they would be in, bordering windows that were open most of the time. And the cost: forty-eight feet of lined drapes? No. I needed more thinking time.

I experimented. I closed all the outside shutters around these windows. This looked good, allowed the breezes in and kept the sun out. But, it turned the house into a darkroom. I couldn't spend a summer in the dark.

A clue came from a flower arrangement I had made from dried grasses. It had been around for a year – didn't look mouldy, didn't look dirty, nothing was eating it, it hadn't faded. Okay, this was the answer. Nature, as usual, solved the problem. What I needed was a drape or curtain made of natural plant material – even the colour would blend with my decor! My search led me to tortoiseshell bamboo blinds: cheap, good colour, impervious to the elements, available in a dozen sizes. In winter I could keep them up, in summer, down. They filtered the light but didn't block it AND they were "islandish," the perfect frame for our glimpses, between the trees, of the ocean. Yep, this was it. And, for a change, it was. They lasted five years, a good record for

Bermuda, good value for the buck. After this length of time, the sun had disintegrated the cord that moved them up and down. But, I was happy. Happy enough to simply replace them with new ones. Or, so I thought.

What a saga that turned out to be. The store that had carried these forever, couldn't get them anymore. In my round-the-island search for another supplier, I heard enough "Hong Kong problem" stories to fill a book. I tried Canada. I tried the States. I needed these windows covered – summer was upon us! I had other problems to solve! Good grief! I bit the bullet and bought mini-blinds.

By the time you read this, tortoiseshells may again be available. If so, try to buy the ones with the dark brown cord. They are of a higher quality than those with the tan cord. One caution: these are not privacy blinds. A peeping Tom, pressed against the window, could see through the slats.

As for the mini-blinds, thankfully, I was smart enough to order the brown ones. Even when they're dirty, they *look* fine. After five years, they still go up and down but the metal mechanism that allows them to tilt open or closed is shot (rust).

HOUSING

I hardly know where to begin. What the heck, let's just dive head first into *reality*. You know that three bedroom house on the beach you've been thinking about? Sorry hon, it ain't gonna happen. Well, just a sec now. Mustn't be hasty. IF you are independently wealthy, it could happen. I think I will take the liberty here, however, to assume you're not in the top 10% of Earth's population.

Do you know how many people want to live in Bermuda? Just imagine. Okay. Now, think 21 square miles. You can see the problem. What happens with challenges such as these? The laws of the universe take over – specifically, the law of supply and demand. Now, what this accomplishes is this: the product *so* desired becomes *so* expensive that only 10% of the global population can afford it. Therefore, it is no longer a problem. Ah, the universe … well … I won't get started on that right now.

Anyway, what all this means is: *you must lower your expectations.* If you don't have a spare *million*, you'll be renting, not buying. (And thank goodness for that. If you were buying, I would need to tell you my 8,000 real estate stories and that would take a very long time.)

The cheapest accommodation I've ever heard of was $500 a month. That was for a bedroom in a family home. The most expensive: $20,000 a month. As you can well imagine, that was for a mansion on the hill by the sea. These, such as they are, are your boundaries.

Single folks generally opt for a studio. This you may know as a bachelor suite. It doesn't actually have a bedroom. Roughly, *very roughly*, you're looking at a starting price of $1,000 per bedroom. So, a studio would be less than that and a three bedroom would start at $3,000.

Now, I know what you're thinking. You'll *need* those extra bedrooms for all the company you'll be having. Correct. BUT (and this is an important point), it's just too expensive for you to maintain a hotel for your guests. They don't know this and will be mightily offended when they find out there's no place for them to bunk in with you. Explain *reality*. Or, better yet, let me do it for you: send them a copy of what you're reading now. Or, cheaper yet, send them the newspaper with the rental prices highlighted! Put them in a nearby guest house. This will save you all sorts of cash and distress.

Keep in mind, you must add telephone and electricity to your rental figure. Then, of course, there are start-up costs, possibly including: the last month's rent, damage deposit and furniture and fixtures.

Are you scared to death yet? Reality tends to do that. As dire as this may sound, everyone finds a home. Even the most hopeless of sorts (and believe me, we've had them here) finds accommodation they can live with. You just have to lower your sights *a bit*.

You are not alone in this. Bermudians go through the same searches for the same rental properties. However, they know what they're dealing with. They know to get on it immediately. They know to tell everyone, *and I mean everyone*, they're looking. They know to leave their contact number with each person they tell. They know to be the first caller on an ad in the paper. They know: be flexible. Now *you know* what you're dealing with and *you know* what they know.

Try to see half a dozen places. Properties here are all so different. Check out the neighbourhood by day and night. Check for bus stops. Use your nose. Mould is detectable. Look for bright, airy and clean. Read your lease carefully. You may have to paint before you move *out*.

Your first home may not be the best you can do, but you'll be under pressure so try not to be too choosy at this point. Once you have the initial relocation stress behind you, you can begin a leisurely search armed with all this new knowledge you've accumulated. At that point, you've survived the big leap. Now, you're a citizen of *Reality*, Bermuda-style.

NAMES

Yes, all Bermuda houses have names. This is an important piece of information to remember when you are noting an address. Often the signs do not carry the house number, but they always have the name, and directions are usually given by names and house colours rather than numbers. Many homes are also listed in the phone book under the house name rather than the occupant. This is especially the case with single women. A smart move, but more than once I have been unable to locate people well-known to me because I didn't know their house name.

Someone should write a book about these names. (No, thank you, I'll pass.) The stories behind many of them are fascinating. One that comes to mind concerns a house named *Anchored*. As the story goes, way back when, a group of college students was sitting around contemplating where life might lead them. By the end of the evening, they had come up with a plan whereby they would be able to find each other come what may. Their plan was this: once they had completed their roaming around the world and settled down, each one of them would name his house *Anchored* and list it in the telephone book as such. As they made their fortunes and travelled around the world, they would make a point of checking the phone book of each city they arrived in to look for this one word. If *Anchored* was listed, they had found one of their original pals. The fellow who related this story to us was one of the *Anchored* team. He reported that, over the years, he had received half a dozen phone calls from the original team in this way. These friends had, in fact, gone on to greater things, lived in countries all over the globe, but had eventually shown up as tourists in Bermuda. Good planning equals great results.

In our case, our house name came within an inch of actually solving a crime. Yes, it did.

Oh boy, this is a long story. First, a little background. When we originally came to Bermuda on our scouting trip, I began thinking of an appropriate name for our house (if, indeed, we ever did find one!). Into this thought process came the decision that the name must include Cassy (our daughter) and Scott (our son) in some way. I was concerned that they feel a part of this new world – a belonging. Cassy, especially, needed constant reassurance that her life had not come to an end. Hubby Paul and I discussed this, combining names in every which way. An ideal solution came quickly. It combined both their names with the eldest coming first. It sounded good. It sounded British. It was easy to spell and to say. It was *Casscott.* Brilliant.

Some years later, we returned from a business trip to Europe to find a very distressed Cassy. In our absence, someone had broken into the house and stolen all of Cassy's and her girlfriend's jewellery. Cassy had called the police and made the report. There was nothing more she could do than to relate the story to us and wait for the police to do their stuff. Sometime later that evening, I picked up the pile of mail (arriving in our absence) and leafed through it. I noticed a letter wrongly addressed and put it to the side. Something was nagging at me. I couldn't put my finger on it, but it was there. While I waited for an answer to break through the surface of my subconscious, I looked at the letter I set aside. It was there. What was it? Then, it bubbled up. Yes, this letter was addressed to an unknown person at our address. This was not unique, but the address contained the name *Casscott.* This was very strange. We had created that name. The chances that someone could have mistakenly put that house name on that letter were non-existent. I picked up the envelope. It held a card of some kind. I immediately suspected fraud. This, coming so close on the heels of the robbery, was also strange. Paul took the letter to the police.

As it turned out, the letter contained a driver's license. This of course, contained a picture and name so our mystery fellow was not difficult to trace. He worked for a company that supplied its employees with trucks. Several of these fellows lived in one house, but only one vehicle can be registered to each dwelling so ... he simply took a look up the street and used the information on our sign to register his truck. We relayed our suspicions to the police. But, we did not stop there.

The letter had come from the bank. We started to put this together. This fellow had used this license for identification at the bank and had left it there by mistake. The bank found it and returned it to the address on the license. He went back to the bank, was told this story and promptly came to our house to recover this I.D. No one was home, but a window, two stories up, was open. With the help of his truck and ladder, he came in through the window to look for his license. He didn't find it, but he did find two piles of jewellery which he took instead. We were ever so impressed with our powers of deduction! We informed the police of our theory.

While all this was going on, our culprit, was not laying idle. A visit from the police must have triggered his flight response. He removed himself from the island. And that was the last we ever heard of it. No doubt Cassy's jewellery is in a pawnshop somewhere in America.

We never did find out if our theory was correct, but WE think so. There is no doubt, however, that this person committed fraud by using our address as his own. Unfortunately, he will never pay for his crime, but I doubt he will ever set foot on this island again.

BUDGET

I had never seen grocery prices like these! Home prices floored me! There were too many digits in these numbers. Definitely sticker shock. I was certain we would be living in poverty. No doubt about it, this was going to be a challenge (another one, good grief!). But, I had a plan.

I had lived with budgets all my life. Yessiree, I knew how to deal with this; a budget would straighten it out pronto! I would just have to make a few adjustments. This country didn't have income tax, adjustment one. Groceries and home prices were double and triple, adjustment two. Homes didn't have furnaces – no natural gas bills to pay – but electricity was double the price, adjustments three and four. Private schools had fees, adjustment five. This went on and on. The point at which adjustments obscured the entire picture had long since passed. Bills I had never before paid were coming in fast and furious. This was not working. So much for plan A.

Plan B. Start from scratch. Establish a new base by listing the expenses month by month for a year. This was a long, drawn-out affair but that base has served us well ever since.

My best advice, in a nutshell: be very careful the first year. You will need all sorts of things you've never needed before. You will be paying bills you've never paid before. If you are not working, you may have the added hassle of living on one less paycheque. Even an occasional dinner out will be twice the cost you thought it would be. While competition has reduced long distance rates dramatically, these calls can still be deadly! Trips home must be worked in. Just take it easy until you know where you're at.

There are bargains to be had. Don't forget the second-hand market. "Early-bird" dinner specials are excellent value. Many entertaining events are free, try those. Pick up one of the tourist publications and see the sights. Take a walk. Join the library. Have a picnic. Spend a day at the beach. Grocery shop on Wednesdays when you receive 5% off your bill as well as the weekly specials. Be aware that a steady stream of guests is very expensive. Buy bus tickets at half the cost of cash fare or, better yet, get a bus pass. This pass also covers ferry usage. Read the paper. Buy pet food by the case if you have a pet; pasta by the case if you have a teenager! Make your OWN iced tea. Make your OWN skim milk!

In general, just pay a little more attention to what you really need. As the story goes, we spend the first forty years of our lives accumulating everything we want and the next forty getting rid of it all. SELL anything and everything you do not use. Remember, if you don't keep it clean, if you don't keep it dry, if you don't keep it moving, it will rust or mould or fade or something! Sell it before that happens. Really, there's very little one needs to be happy.

CHAPTER THREE

A Matter of Principle

CONTROLS

"What do you mean – 'I need a permit'?"

Man has the tendency to destroy that which he values most highly. Luckily, nature has compensated for this by providing us with a superior brain, capable of insight, planning and the power to reason. Over the centuries, Bermuda's brains have put in place sufficient controls to ensure that man's innate capacity to destroy is checked. As early as 1616, laws were passed to protect Bermuda's birds, specifically, the cahow. In this regard, Bermuda made history by issuing the first conservation laws in the New World. In 1620, turtles also came under this umbrella with conservation and preservation continuing since.

At first, you will find this most frustrating, but think for a moment. Try and put this in perspective. Bermuda is a country of twenty-one square miles, a mere dot in the ocean. On this dot live 63,000 people. Many, many countries thousands of times larger are reeling from the effects of human abuse and misuse. These controls are necessary, positive, mandatory. They ensure the survival of the quality of life for which Bermuda is famous and the island thrives on a Victorian sense of law and order.

The roads and parking lots simply cannot accommodate four cars per family. One car per household is the law. (Rental cars are not permitted.) Narrow, winding streets cannot handle speeds of 60 miles per hour (20 is the speed limit) or vehicles the size of stretch limousines (car length, width and engine size are strictly controlled). City merchants, compressed into several square blocks, cannot accommodate four cruise ships disgorging thousands of passengers at once. I am reminded of a cruise we took to another island. We couldn't get into the stores; three ships had arrived before us. We couldn't part with our money; we didn't even try. Bermudians know that quality is inversely related to quantity. Cruise ship arrivals are restricted. Four cruise ships on Front Street would create chaos.

Neon signs, billboards, gambling and guns are all prohibited, for obvious reasons.

Work permits, as well as status awards, are limited. Everyone wants to live in paradise. Even the spouse of a Bermudian must fulfill both a residence and length of marriage requirement before status is granted. Do not feel put out by this; you already have a country. Bermudians deserve first rights to theirs.

Let's suppose you were posted overseas for two years. At the end of this period, you decided to return home, settle down, put down some roots. You went house hunting for a little place all your own. Then, you found out, you couldn't buy a house – there wasn't a house to be had. The Bermudians bought them all. Then, you went looking for employment. No luck here either. Every job you wanted was taken – by a Bermudian. In your country or mine, this couldn't happen. In Bermuda it could, and would, without controls.

While Bermuda may have a niche for your husband to fill, this does not necessarily extend to you. Unless there is a distinct shortage of your particular talents, it is highly unlikely that you too will find employment. You may even be required to sign a waiver stating that you will not seek work. You must understand and accept this – before you arrive. If the term "housewife" sends chills up your spine, reconsider your decision to move, reassess your priorities.

Whatever your plans, keep in mind that you will probably need a permit. Be safe, check first. One lady I knew married her boyfriend so she could accompany him here. For six months she searched for a job. Then, she left ... left the job search ... left Bermuda ... left her husband. Such a waste!

BANKING

I'm going to address this topic separately because it has the potential to make you REALLY, REALLY cranky. But, if you pay close attention, you'll be spared. If you don't ... well ... prepare for an *ordeal*. To open your first Bermuda bank account requires everything but your first-born son. I always know when our newly hired guests have been through this procedure – they return here with smoke coming out of their ears. Well, *really*, if they would have *told* me they were opening their account, I would have *explained*.

The following should accompany you on your first bank visit: a letter of reference from your previous bank, a character reference, your passport, your work permit, at least $50 to deposit in your new account AND enough patience to keep you calm while THEY sort through all this stuff. This should be one of the first things you get going on when you arrive. It may take two weeks to clear foreign drafts and several days before you can access your account and cash cheques.

As aggravating as all this may be, it is exactly this kind of thoroughness that has kept Bermuda out of international financial scandals; it is this that has kept her reputation blue chip. Really, the bank doesn't know you from a hole in the ground. If, for whatever reason, you are dealing in large numbers, be prepared to justify your banking transactions. Money laundering is NOT one of our problems and these controls ensure it won't be.

While I have you gathering papers together, I offer a few more suggestions to simplify your life. Get a letter from your past car insurance company stating what a good driver you are (this is worth the time – a no-claims discount can save you more than half on your premium). To the telephone company, take your passport and your landlord's name and contact number. To the electricity company, take your passport, $150 deposit and either the name of the previous tenant or the meter number.

Your past credit record means nothing here. (Isn't THAT weird? It's like your old driver's license – no one cares that you're authorized to drive anywhere in the WORLD – you still need a *Bermuda* driver's license to toodle around at 20 mph on 21 square miles.) Now, you would think, with the stack of papers you must keep presenting to accomplish *anything,* your credit record would certainly be something worth looking into. Guess not. You can get a Bermuda credit card BUT it will have a $500 limit. If you travel, $500 just won't cut it. Hang on to your old credit cards from home.

SPEED & TIME

"Girl, why you so gribble? Relax, have a rum swizzle."

An oft quoted saying, "Bermuda is another world", is no more apt than in regards to time. This phenomenon is so entrenched that even newcomers quickly learn that the Bermuda clock is somewhere between an hour and a week behind all others. Nine o'clock, Monday morning and tomorrow most likely means noon, Wednesday and next week! It is in your best interest to accept this immediately and save yourself a lot of frustration. Patience is required in the pursuit of services of any kind. Finding a repairman is the first challenge. Actually getting him to your home is the second. Getting the job completed is the third. After dozens of experiences, I determined that it is the third phone call that brings results. Having left a fast track, double-time, on-call sales career, this took some getting used to ... about two years.

Both the climate and the friendliness of Bermudians foster this attitude towards time. While Bill, the mason, may have every intention of arriving at nine, he will meet, on his way, Bob, then Tom, then Joe. It is, after all, only common courtesy that he inquire of each as to the health of their mother, aunt and sister, discuss the wedding of last weekend and express his views on the latest news, weather and sports happenings. By this time it has begun to rain, so he must then enclose his equipment, and himself, in plastic of some sort. As he is doing this, he notices that he is right next door to the paint shop. Well! He may as well pick up that gallon of paint he's been planning to buy. Who knows when he'll get up this way again, might as well SAVE some time! While he's attending to that, it stops raining, the sun comes out and it's as hot as the dickens. Good grief, who can rush in this heat? Then there's Jacob. He has three girlfriends in three parishes. The problem is, he has children from each of these women and it's *his duty* to see that they ALL get to school on time. What a guy! Then there's Byron. He has three jobs (as many Bermudians do) and has never been on time for anything. And so it goes. After my first year here, I stopped asking the various workmen why they were so late. I simply could not listen to one more of these recitations.

If needed supplies are being ordered for you, double the stated delivery time. In all fairness, let me state that so many factors are at play here that it is foolhardy to expect that the manufacturer, trucker, shipper, weather, dock workers, customs agents, distributors and retailer can possibly co-ordinate all their schedules to bring in your order on the specified date. This list of accomplices also helps explain why goods are expensive here. Bermuda must import more than 90% of the goods consumed on the island. With this is mind, the variety and abundance available is truly amazing.

YOU MUST SLOW DOWN. Bermudians will not speed up to your pace. This could be the reason Bermudians live so long. I remember being amazed at the age of the store clerks when I first arrived. It seemed six out of every dozen had passed retirement age! I felt sorry for these people, assuming that these poor old souls had to drag themselves into work each day just to pay their bills. There was no reason to

46

pity them. They were alert, alive and active. They had a reason to get up in the morning; they were self-sufficient. They met and conversed and laughed and sang with each other all day. (This is how you tell a Bermudian – he's the one singing!) Not surprisingly, these old-timers knew their products inside out. They rode motorbikes to work. These were people to envy and admire. Recently, I had my groceries packed by an elderly lady who had served me for years at one of the downtown department stores. I asked her why she had switched jobs and she replied that *they* thought she should retire. Obviously, she didn't! Perhaps, it is the beauty of their island home or the lack of pollution or one of the dozen other advantages Bermudian life offers, but I think it's the relaxed pace of life here that allows this section of society to remain vibrant and productive and, most of all, pleasant. Indeed, it allows all who live here the time to be friendly.

However, efficiency withers in this environment – you can't have both. If the lady ahead of you at the checkout counter is known to the cashier, allow them time for their chit-chat. Don't get mad; it doesn't work and simply highlights the fact that you're new here. I speak from experience. More than once, I've had a hand laid on my shoulder and heard a calm voice say, "Girl, why you so gribble? Relax, have a rum swizzle." And, believe me, I've had my share of them.

LANGUAGE

Way back when, at the start of my Bermudian life, I kept hearing conversations about someone being *axed*. Knowing this was a civilized country where purse snatching was news, I knew it couldn't be possible that people were being cut in pieces on a regular basis. Neither could I understand why everyone kept calling me *girl*. Or *hon* or *sweetheart*. I read in the newspaper that a fellow had been arrested because he was *full hot*. The mason, who preceded every sentence with, *"Um ... um ..."*, told me he had to leave early to attend to his *her*. No doubt, because of the strange look on my face, he then inquired, "Are you *waxed?*" Rather than deal with his impossible questions, I asked one myself, "Where is your helper today?" He replied, "Took *licks* last evenin', gave him an *attitude*". When I had lunch with my Bermudian friend, she asked if I would like a *purr*. At my questioning look she said, "Well, maybe you

47

would prefer a *burr.*" I was forever hearing a word that sounded like *gribble.* Each time I asked a question about this country, I was told it had something to do with *guvmit.* I didn't have a clue what any of these people were talking about.

What was needed here was time, lots of time. Time for me to hear these words often enough that I could grasp their meaning from context. Paul could have been helpful with this but by the time he got home, I had usually forgotten the pronunciation of these puzzling expressions. Time did, in fact, answer my questions.

Ninety percent of the people, ninety percent of the time, speak excellent English. However, I have included this story because, sooner or later, you will come into contact with older Bermudians, especially workmen, who speak this way. To help you along a bit, I will translate. *Axed* is asked. *Girl, hon* and *sweetheart* simply denote friendliness. *Full hot* translates to drunk; *half-hot,* is therefore half-drunk. *Um...um...* means the speaker needs several seconds to collect his thoughts. *Her* is hair. *Waxed* is vexed, which means angry. When someone *took licks,* he lost a fight – a good reason, I suppose, for having *an attitude* (being out of sorts) that day. *Purr* is pear and *burr* is beer. This is particularly confusing as the "air" sound is treated the same way has the "ear" sound. *Gribble* is slang for disagreeable. *Guvmit* is government and is, of course, blamed for everything.

While I was getting to the bottom of all this, I felt I should wear a sign around my neck stating that the wearer does not speak *Bermewjan.* This, of course, may have been offensive. The concern about this (causing offense) was also the reason it took me so long to decipher these words. I had to be comfortable enough with the speaker to explain that I didn't know what in the world he was talking about. The strange thing was, while all this was going on, everyone knew exactly what I was saying. I was also amazed that everyone knew I was Canadian. Each time I questioned them about this, they responded it was MY funny way of talking that gave me away!

At this time, there is a booklet available to solve these riddles for you. It's called *Bermewjan Vurds* (Bermudian Words) which just goes to show that someone, besides me, feels translation is necessary.

GOOD MORNING

"Pardon me?" Cassy said. I repeated, "I'm going to town to practise my 'Good mornings'."

The greeting, "Howdy!", does not wash here. Neither does hello or hi. Good morning, good afternoon and good evening are the acceptable greetings, preferably followed by – and how are you today? This takes some getting used to. First of all, it's quite a mouthful compared to hi; secondly, it requires a quick calculation of time (is it 11 a.m. or past noon?). A smile WITH eye contact completes the greeting. This all seems like a lot of fuss for the purchase of one 30-cent stamp!

For a female, raised in a large city, chatting with strangers was not only a forbidden but a dangerous practice. This about-face took some effort. But, practice makes perfect and practise I did. I'm still at it.

While I'm on this topic, let me also mention construction workers. Every "big city" woman has experienced walking past a construction site. In case you happen to be a small town girl, I will explain. The scenario goes something like this. On her way to a particular destination, a female passes a group of men working on a building. Upon sighting her, the air is filled with unmistakable requests such as, "Hey baby, why don't you sashay over here?" or "Cold, Sugar? I got something that will warm you up" or "Step into my parlour, Sweet Stuff, I want to be a fly." Looking straight ahead, feigning deafness, the recipient of these remarks hurries away from these wanton rogues.

In Bermuda, men are every bit as masculine but ... they are ever so proper about it. They have developed a subtle and cunning strategy (generally a female tactic) allowing an effective coup. Instead of stomping off in a huff, the woman will automatically smile. Yes, she will! How can you be rude to the fellow who asks, "Did your President send you over here to pretty up our island?" or "Does your husband know what a lucky man he is?" Do you know what you just did? You smiled. Twice. I rest my case.

THANK YOU

It was to be my first introduction to Paul's family. The stage was set; we were going off to meet Great Aunt Hilda. Good grief.

These first meetings are always stressful. What to wear? What to say? How to play it? Paul was never helpful in these situations. He thought I was perfect. Couple this with his optimistic attitude about EVERYTHING in life and I was left explaining my "preparation is key" speech, to myself.

Okay. What did I know? Paul and Hilda had an endearing relationship; that had to mean she was a special lady. She was a great aunt; that meant she was pretty old. It was comforting to recall that I had quite a bit of experience with these gals born at the turn of the century. Through them I learned that many of the famous jokes about "old maids" were true: One old maid to the other, "Don't let them write 'Miss' on my grave, I haven't missed as much as some may think!" These ladies had lived near a hundred years! What HADN'T they seen? If I played the "I'm the perfect little bride for your perfect little nephew" role, would this be an insult to her intelligence? But, then again, my completely natural, brutally honest manner had landed me in the soup more than once. Hmm, what to do? Well ... all right ... I'd just have to play it by ear.

Great Aunt Hilda was a darlin' ... as gracious a lady as I've ever met. She was a tiny little bit of a thing; I felt like an Amazon next to her. She welcomed me with open arms and cried when we left. My compassion for her rose to nuclear heights when she explained her early life. She was a teenage bride. Shortly after her marriage, her husband went off to sea, as was the custom for young men at the time. That was the last time she saw him. Think about that for a moment. The loss ... the uncertainty ... her pain must have been incredible. When I met her, some sixty years later, she was still waiting. She had never married again. My heart ached for her. But, she wasn't bitter; she wasn't angry. On the contrary, she was so pleasant, so courteous, I could hardly stand it. Every one of her sentences began or ended with "thank you". I'm not kidding! I had no idea what I was doing or saying that made her so grateful. A dozen times, I asked Paul why she did this. He didn't know. I didn't know. I know now. Great Aunt Hilda was Bermudian. Therein lies the answer.

When I moved here, this thank you business began again. Everyone was saying it – constantly. The lady in front of me at the post office said thank you six times, for one stamp. Everyone on the bus thanked the bus driver when they got off. Every shopper thanked the cashier as they left the store – even when they didn't buy anything! It was a mystery to me, but I figured I'd better join in. I suggest you do the same. When in Rome ....

It becomes a habit quite quickly and there's certainly nothing wrong with a little extra courtesy in this world, Lord knows we need it. However, I must admit, I get some pretty weird looks when I get off the bus in Glasgow. The driver can't imagine why on earth I'm saying *thank you.*

RESPECT

"I would have thought, you would have taught your children more respect," my friend said to me.

I'm sure it was a difficult phone call to make. My friend was obviously distressed and insulted. She explained that Scott had noticed her in the grocery store and said, "Hi, Sarah." Clearly, this was not acceptable to her, but, try as I might, I could not grasp the problem. After more discussion, I began to make it out.

It was not my custom to be formal. I subconsciously assume I'm in trouble of some sort when I'm addressed as *Mrs. Caswell* – not unlike angry Mother Jones addressing naughty little Debbie with "Deborah Ann Jones, have you been warming your slippers in the toaster again?"

Diplomacy and tact. If you are in possession of these qualities, bring them with you. They will prove invaluable here.

Somewhat like Amsterdam, New York or Montreal, Bermuda is a melting pot of values, principles and beliefs from cultures around the world. This is something to keep in mind when joining social circles or making new friends. While I consider the use of a given name friendly, some consider it too familiar. Avoid this problem; simply address each new acquaintance as Mr. or Ms. and their surname. If this is not their preference, they will tell you.

I would like to tell you that I am much more comfortable with just plain *Tracey*! This always proves a problem for the workmen at Casscott.

They introduce themselves to me by their given names, I respond in kind, but, to date, not one of them has ever called me *Tracey* – it's always *Mrs. Caswell*. Mama taught them well.

Before I leave the subject of respect, let me note that Bermudians are not comfortable with the term *native*. When you feel a need to use this word, substitute *local* instead.

Let me also mention taxi drivers. They are not your typical recently arrived immigrant, as is usually the case elsewhere. This is a highly regarded profession in Bermuda – many of these taxi drivers are independently wealthy!

BEHAVIOUR

June 1991

A business professional and a 51-year-old father of three looked around the beach. He couldn't see a soul. It was suppertime, probably most people were home doing just that, "suppering". There were some large rocks to hide behind if need be, so he stripped and went for a swim in the ocean. What he did not see was an off-duty policeman who did, in fact, see him.

The General Manager of a major corporation for a period of four years, this gentleman, an expatriate, was highly respected for his contributions to the island. He had never been in trouble before and reportedly was deeply embarrassed by his admitted lack of judgement this day. To show his remorse he offered a generous donation to one of the island's charities.

The following month, news bulletins and reports recorded that he had received a letter from Immigration stating that his work permit would not be renewed. The letter also stated that he should settle his affairs by the end of August. Skinny-dipping on a public beach in Bermuda is a serious affair.

Bermudians, as a whole, are a highly moral and religious group. (Yes, this is why there is a church on every corner.) They will turn in a found wallet, contents intact. As a guest in their home, they expect you to hold yourself to the same high standards. Do not underestimate the gravity of misdemeanors; do not break the law either legally or morally; do not forget to pay your rent. Do not even THINK of bucking the system. You will lose. I have never heard of a place with such vigilant traffic wardens. Somehow they know when every car, in every parking lot and on every street, should be gone. If you park illegally, you WILL get a ticket. If you speed, it could be worse – you could lose your licence.

Let the true story above serve as your guide. While there was quite an outcry to "save" the gentleman concerned, he does not reside here anymore.

CHARACTERS

In other countries, they're called *bums* or *drunks*. In ever-so-civilized Bermuda, they're *characters* or *rummies*. You will see them often, engaged in passionate conversations with invisible beings. Their language may not be to your liking, but they are basically harmless. Actually, a few are rich and famous; magazine and news articles have told their story. The first one I saw was Tommy "Wardrobe" Tucker – a tall, dark, elderly fellow. He was a familiar sight around Hamilton, slowly walk/riding his bicycle, loaded down with a world of second-hand goods. Quite a stir was created when he won a trip to Paris in a raffle. First, he was besieged with responses to his ad for a guardian to accompany him on the trip. Then, his multiple layers of pants had to be CUT OFF to enable the hospital staff to give him a bath. Then, he needed a passport and new clothes. One must assume all this was simply more fuss than Tommy could deal with. In the end, he backed out. Several years later, he passed away.

On the other side of the scale is an immaculate, straw-hatted, religious, elderly gentleman by the name of Johnny Barnes. His mission is to create smiles and there's a whole lot of smilin' goin' on between 5:30 and 10:00 a.m. Between these hours, Monday to Friday, rain or shine, Johnny stands at the Crow Lane roundabout, waving his arms and greeting all those who pass with, "Hello darling, I love you" or "Don't forget we love you now. Have a beautiful day." In Bermuda, he is a goodwill ambassador. Magazines and newspapers tell his story too; posters display his picture; invitations to important events come his way. HE is definitely famous. You'll see him and hear him and smile. You may see him twice, moments apart, in two locations – first, in the flesh; a little further on, in bronze. Well, I told you he was famous! A statue of him was commissioned, created and placed at the entrance to Hamilton, just past where he stands in the morning. Honestly, I am not making this up. Smiles are honoured in Bermuda. Perhaps, if we were all a little less suspicious of the *weird folks* we encounter, we would find that they too are just as special as Johnny.

CAUCASIAN

Cassy was not having a good day. It was about to get worse.

"I'm tired. I don't want to go to town. I just want my hair cut," she said. I replied. "Look in the phone book, find a hairdresser close by and give her a call." That, she did.

The conversation went as follows: Cassy: Can I make an appointment for a haircut today? Hairdresser: Are you Caucasian? Cassy, flustered: Well ... no ... I'm Canadian.

I thought this was HILARIOUS. Cassy did not. The conversation ended with an abrupt statement: "I don't do Caucasian hair." Then, the stylist hung up.

You will occasionally meet with situations like this. Perhaps, this woman simply did not feel comfortable or qualified to deal with hair unlike that of her usual clientele. Perhaps, this was a case of clear-cut prejudice. It doesn't matter. The important point here is how you handle such predicaments. I will relate the same speech I gave my daughter that day.

This is life – here and everywhere else. Religion, economic status, ethnic origin, political views and yes, skin colour, are but a few of the subjects capable of inducing friction, misunderstanding and severe differences of opinion. This would be man's greatest accomplishment: to exist happily within his own species. Why is this so difficult? Prejudice is such a useless emotion. Rise above it.

A battle requires an opponent. Don't be one. When you meet with this sort of aggression, try this: Soften your eyes and say, "I'm sorry you feel that way." And then, WALK AWAY.

CHAPTER FOUR

Incredible Edibles

VEGETABLES

I was becoming famous – for throwing fits in grocery stores. I was at it again. "How can you NOT have carrots? What kind of a store is this anyway? Why is there an embargo on CARROTS? Four months without carrots – impossible!" Wisely, the produce manager didn't even try to answer the questions from this one-person firing squad. (He was probably married and knew better.) His thoughts were in his eyes, "Another one of them crazy foreigners." I needed carrots. I needed a universally accepted vegetable. I needed the texture, the shape, the colour, for my plate presentation. I was having a dinner party for heaven's sake! This was obviously *another* one of those days I should have gone to the Aquarium.

Embargoes are in effect for two reasons: to ensure a full market for the Bermuda-grown crop and to ensure that pests, particular to that food, have no chance to establish themselves here. Sensible enough when you think about it. I hadn't. I never had reason to. This was now number 1042 in that category which brings me to my next recommendation: when planning a menu, plan for alternatives and check the stores before you carve it in stone.

Now, where was I? Oh yes, carrots. Before I leave this subject, let me say that these little guys are the fattest and shortest ones you've ever seen! This results from the fact that Bermuda's soil, on average, is only four inches deep. Another amazing statistic.

Potatoes, onions, corn, green beans, pumpkin and kale are just a few of the dozens of vegetables grown here. Bermuda onions were a major export in the late 1800's. They were SO popular in the New York market that Bermudians became known as "Onions". Competition from American farmers, import duty and a reduction of available farming land ended this trade in the 1930's but the nickname stuck and is still in regular use today.

Pumpkin, as far as I knew, was only eaten in pie. After years of gentle nudging from a friend, I started to put it in soups and stews and sauces. Now I love it this way. A few more years and I'm sure I will be able to eat it "straight!" Kale is a large, leafy, dark green vegetable. I am adjusting to this one too. In soup, it's fine. Both kale and pumpkin are unbelievably nutritious. I HAVE to use them. I am constantly dealing with the challenge of incorporating six servings of fruit and vegetables into our diet each day. With this in mind, I must have variety. A vegetable soup, salad or sauce goes a long way to meeting this goal.

It would be well worth your while to seek out a farmer. The demand for Bermuda produce far outstrips the supply. Many varieties never make it to the grocery store. If you are not working, you'll have time to mess with all this fresh stuff and, for the price you'll be paying, you may as well have the best. It may take you awhile to meet a farmer. It won't take you long to meet friends. And friends have friends who have friends. Friends share.

At some point, you will be given a food that completely baffles you. For me, this was christophene. "What IS this?" I said to my pal. She told me the name and then, as is wont to happen with chit-chat, we went off on another topic. I went home with a bag of light green, pear-shaped, hard things with a name I couldn't even spell. Now, WHAT was I going to do with these little devils? Ho hum, more research. I searched through twelve cookbooks and the encyclopedia for information. Do I peel them? Cook them? How? How long? Are they ripe? Are they supposed to be ripe? I was getting nowhere fast on this search. I called my friend and then followed her instructions. All the fuss wasn't worth it. They tasted like boiled water! But, I didn't give up (I still had three left). I bought a Bermuda cookbook and found a recipe using bread crumbs, cheese, milk and spices – bound to taste good. However, my group and I decided it still wasn't worth the trouble. If you are the recipient of the same gift and have the same experience, put them in a soup or stew, they just get lost in there. For times like these, a couple of Bermuda cookbooks will prove invaluable. Buy them. Try some of the local dishes.

I was aware that some of these unfamiliar foods required special procedures or ripening to a certain stage before eating. Cassava and ackees come to mind. Be wary of foods you are not familiar with. Seek out the knowledge of a Bermudian or call the Department of Agriculture. Many plants are poisonous. Some are completely confusing. Stinging nettles do just that, sting, upon skin contact. It would seem this is not a good food choice. However, the young shoots are a vegetable and the leaves have been used for tea in Europe for centuries. Amazing.

FRUIT

A Bermuda-grown orange, lemon or grapefruit is a prize worth seeking out. The exterior may put you off, being covered in black splotches, but, not to worry, the interior holds the sweetest, juiciest fruit you've ever eaten. Watch for them around Christmas.

Loquats, Surinam cherries, Natal plums and bay grapes are fruits found growing wild all over the island. These are primarily used for jam, although a liqueur, *Bermuda Gold*, is made from loquats – little, yellow, oval-shaped fruits which are delicious raw and can be made into cakes, pies and chutney. Look for them in February and March. These months are a good time to be cooking but be warned: loquats are a pain to cook with. Each one contains several huge seeds so you need LOTS of them. They oxidize (like apples) so you must work fast AND with lemon juice. We have several loquat trees. Of course, I HAD to find a use for them. After years of experimentation, I realized, what I needed to do was to find a very similar fruit and then, a recipe book for that fruit. I settled on peaches. Eventually, I got to Georgia, the peach capital of the world. I scoured the stores. All I could find were huge cookbooks with a peach recipe here and there. Nope, didn't need that. As we were about to board the plane home, I found a $6 peach cookbook in the airport gift shop. Never say die.

Surinam cherries grow on a dense, evergreen hedge. In late Spring, the yellow, then orange, then red, grooved, lantern-looking berries appear. Wait until they are a deep red and then try them. They have a spicy, sweet, sour taste. I don't like them myself.

Natal plums grow on a beautiful deep green leafy hedge. Be wary: the stems have strong, spiked thorns that can puncture flesh in an instant. Grown under windows, they prove an effective deterrent to thieves. The white flowers of this plant are delicate and fragrant; the fruit is deep red, plum-like and yummy. Generally, if the juice or sap of a plant is white, it should not be eaten. This fruit breaks that rule. Another rule to keep in mind: do not assume a food is safe because birds eat it; their digestive system is different than ours. This breaks MY general rule of looking to nature for the answers. Why must there always be exceptions? No wonder we're all so confused.

Bay grape trees grow profusely along the South Shore. They are incredibly hardy with leathery leaves resistant to sun, salt, sand and wind. Bunches of green, then purple grapes hang from the thick branches. They are edible when purple but I don't like these either. Best to put them in a jam unless you like this exotic taste. If you like the Surinams, you might like these.

I spend a lot of time messing about with pawpaw. This is actually papaya. I do this because it is so nutrition-packed AND I just happen to have a gazillion of them in my yard. Bermudians tend to eat them green, as a vegetable. I, however, let them ripen to orange and eat them as a raw fruit. Quite honestly, I don't like the taste. But, how does one allow wild, homegrown, unadulterated fruit, loaded with vitamins A and C plus potassium, calcium and fiber, to rot on the ground? I mean, really, even the seeds are edible! They have a peppery, astringent taste – good in salads when dried and ground. In old Bermuda, pawpaw juice was used for ringworm and warts. Several older Bermudians have also told me pawpaws bring down blood pressure and help digestion. All of this is quite possible. The fruit contains the enzyme papain. Papain breaks down protein. It is, therefore, an excellent meat tenderizer AND exfoliant. Now, REALLY, how could I let this wonder fruit go to waste?

Locust-and-Wild-Honey or *Monstera deliciosa* is the delight of our tourists. This cucumber-sized and -shaped fruit takes forever to grow, ripens by the inch and is eaten one kernel at a time – truly the fussiest fruit I've ever known. But, it is so delicious. The taste compares to a combination of banana, pineapple and almond. When we have guests arriving, I place one of them in a paper bag in a dark cupboard for a week. This hastens the ripening process. I can't forget it's in there as the fragrance is wonderful, permeating the kitchen as it becomes ready to eat. We have had guests from all over the world, but not once has anyone seen, or heard of – much less tasted – this fruit. We have lots of fun with it. Look for what you know as philodendron leaves, VERY BIG philodendron leaves. Depending on the season, you may see large, white, leathery flowers. If that time has passed and the flowers have dried and dropped away, you will note what appears to be a deep green cobs of corn. This is the fruit in some stage of its ten-month ripening process. If the tiny, outer, hexagonal plates have begun to peel back, the PEELED part is ready to eat. Do not be tempted to eat the unpeeled portion as it contains a mild acid (feels like crystals in your mouth). Nature will show you how much you can have each day – she's fussy with this treat!

Bananas are abundant. They are of a dwarf variety, smaller than the ones you're probably most familiar with. They're also sweeter. The ripening process is a bit different too. You will notice that even when the skin begins to turn black, the fruit is still in good shape. Don't throw out these blackened bananas until you have checked inside. In summer, bananas do not turn yellow so go by feel to determine whether they are ripe. With bananas it's feast or famine around here. I have none, then I have four dozen. In feast times they go into milkshakes and banana bread. Once ripened, you can place them in the fridge to preserve them for a few more days. Peeled bananas can be frozen in plastic bags and make nutritious, natural "popsicles" for children – plain or dipped in chocolate.

We had a peach tree so I know they grow here too. I'm afraid I fatally mutilated our tree by poor pruning. Gardening is not my forte. If you don't know what you're doing (and obviously I don't), let the professionals deal with your fruit trees.

Just before I leave this topic, let me mention an incident that happened not only to me, but to another friend. We both purchased a whole watermelon. When I put the knife in mine – it exploded! My kitchen was covered in sloppy red slime, and so was I. The same thing happened to my friend. We theorized that this fruit had been too long off the vine, and the heat of the summer had caused the over-ripened fruit to produce a gas under pressure. When the tip of the knife created a small opening, the gas and the contents burst forth. You can imagine how I spent the rest of that day. So ... be wary of specials on whole watermelons.

CUISINE

"Who, on earth, is Hoppin' John?"

A barrage of unfamiliar words and names will come at you from all directions when you first arrive. Generally, these words are prefaced with, "Do you like ... ?" I had no idea whether I liked him or not; I never met the man.

Hoppin' John is not one of Bermuda's strange characters. It's a black-eyed peas and rice dish. Cassava pie is a Christmas and Easter specialty made with meat, sugar and cassava root (loaded with calories). Pawpaw Montespan is a meat, cheese and unripe papaya (pawpaw) casserole. Fish cakes, another Easter treat, are fried patties of mashed potatoes, onions, parsley and salted codfish. Codfish with potatoes, bananas, avocados and/or tomatoes is a popular Sunday breakfast. Curried mussel, beef or chicken pies form part of every Bermuda menu.

Two soups top the specialties list: fish chowder and red bean. Grandma threw a fit in a restaurant when she was served fish chowder. She kept telling the waiter that chowder is made with cream. This one isn't. The broth is made with fish and vegetables, and is not complete without the addition of a dash (or splash) of black rum and sherry peppers. Sherry peppers are exactly that – sherry, flavored by small, red, hot peppers. Red bean soup is a hearty blend of kidney beans, kale, potatoes, carrots and chourico. Chourico, pronounced in every possible way, including "shadeesh", is a hot, spicy Portuguese sausage.

Having arrived from beef, cheese and milk country, I was wary of all these new and different taste sensations. If you are the same, I encourage you to try them. If you don't like them, fine, that's over with. Many you will enjoy. Cassava pie was a tough one for me to get into. It seemed to me that a pie should be either meat or sweet, but not both. I kept sampling it though, trying to figure out what all the fuss was about. Now I look forward to my Christmas and Easter slice.

I knew what allspice was, had used it for years. But, I didn't know *the story* and I didn't know my yard was producing it. I had "spice trees" which produced a purple berry that some of my Bermudian friends enjoyed. Mom, a Canadian, returning from a Jamaican tour, informed me that these were allspice berries. I checked the encyclopedia. She was right. Before ripening to the purple color, these berries are a brown-gold. From these brown-gold berries, allspice is made. These trees grow everywhere on the island and can be distinguished by the smell of a broken leaf – the aroma is that of cloves. Well, obviously the aroma must be that of allspice but every time I have someone guess, they say cloves. Hmm, I wonder if they could be interchangeable in recipes?

As well as allspice, half the plant family grows in our yard. Occasionally, I give tourists a one-hour tour and tell them everything I know about the plants in *our jungle*. This isn't much, but it's volumes more than I knew when I arrived. In a food shortage, I'm certain I could keep us fed for months!

In preparation for this unlikely eventuality, I've researched; I've experimented. Fennel has kept me quite busy. From this wild herb, I've made tea, sauce, soup and salad. It's great with fish. From nettles, I've made tea. From nasturtiums, I've made soups and salads. With spice berries or cedar berries I've enhanced red meat gravies. Yesterday, I read that the flower petals of the Spanish Bayonet plant are edible. This plant just happens to be blooming profusely on South Shore at the moment so when we went on our nightly walk last night, I ate one. Yuk! I must admit that my family does not look forward to these experimental days. I don't tell them anymore! It seems a crime to have natural, fresh ingredients growing wild outside the back door and not do SOMETHING with them. In bumper crop years, I've created facials and hair conditioners of avocados and papaya. Cassy was not very impressed with these episodes either – messy, messy. But, I explained, papaya is a great exfoliator; avocado is a fabulous moisturizer. She didn't care; she wanted this junk off her face; she wanted to get out of the kitchen and she wanted me to leave her alone. Well, it WAS a novel way to spend an evening.

MILK

With the carrot episode fresh in my mind, I thought I had best check first. The answer: "Yes, we have milk. Would you like red, blue, green, pink or brown?"

Good grief! Not again! Milk! White milk! From cows! How complicated could that be? Why were they doing this to me?

I had to get to the bottom of this one quickly. Having arrived from cow country with two children in tow, milk was not something I was prepared to mess with. I called the local dairy. I asked to speak with the chemist. I got the milk story.

Blue signifies whole milk. Brown, sensibly enough, is chocolate milk. The pink and white container with blue writing is 2% fresh milk. Are you confused yet? The latter is probably the one you want. The green container is skim milk and all the rest are milks with varying degrees of fat. Sounds okay so far, right? Here's the kicker. These milks are made from skim milk powder. Then, *vegetable oil* is added to bring it up to the fat content desired – 1%, 2% etc. No wonder my tea had an extra layer on top! No wonder it didn't taste like milk. Vegetable oil in my tea was something I could do without and I could put water in skim milk powder myself. This I have done since. If you also make this choice, remember to make up your milk a day ahead. It needs to "bloom". No, I can't actually explain that but, trust me, it *needs* to do this. Another benefit of making your own: you can make it as strong as you like – a great way to get more calcium: use less water.

I often take our cottage guests grocery shopping when they arrive. As they approach the checkout counter, milk is the first thing I look for. If I don't, experience has shown this scenario will follow: the guest will appear at my back door; he will be holding a quart of red milk; he will say, "Ah, Tracey ... there seems to be a problem here". Innkeeper job 61 – sort out the milk situation.

PACKERS

From a very young age, Scott was a social creature. Not one to find pleasure in quiet pursuits, he was always with people, in the action and, hopefully, making money. At the tender age of eight, he was serving up slurpies at our community convenience store. By the age of twelve, there was no holding him back. By this time we had been in Bermuda one year and he absolutely insisted on working part-time. We checked the market for possible jobs for a twelve-year-old. And, we found one. His first day on the job was one none of us will ever forget. He worked twelve hours; his feet were numb; he made fifty dollars! He was in seventh heaven! He was rich! This was also the day three tornadoes hit the island.

No, don't panic. Tornadoes seldom hit. This is the only time I recall them doing any damage. No, no one died. As far as I know, no one was even hurt.

Okay, where was I? Oh yes. After this eventful day, Scott was, officially, a grocery packer. And he remained at this job for five years. Therefore, I have first-hand (second-hand?) information about this occupation.

The grocery stores employ student packers at a salary of a dollar a day. The balance of their wages comes from tips. Tipping is always a tricky business, so I will give you some guidelines. Fifty cents a bag is now standard. As you will discover, a quarter, or for that matter, a dollar, doesn't go far in Bermuda. The job of a packer is to load your groceries into the bags, put the bags in a cart, take them to your car and unload them. A packer should be conscientious – strawberries, mushrooms and bread should end up at the top of the bag, not at the bottom. He (or she) should also smile occasionally and he should load the bags into the car properly. If he does all this, he should be rewarded. At Christmas, Easter or whenever these fellows are rushed of their feet, consider giving more.

Some stores employ mentally challenged packers. Be patient with them; they are doing their best to be productive individuals.

COOKING

For three of my teenage years, I lived with Grandma. Grandma was a cook throughout World War II in the Canadian Air Force. I tried to learn a fraction of what she knew. I really tried. However, she never could quite grasp the fact that I had not attended the chef training classes of 1942 with her. Learning to cook from Grandma was a most frustrating business. When I asked for the recipe for her fabulous plum pudding, she said, "Make a cake batter and add plums." This was a typical explanation of all her recipes. If I asked the size of pan to use, she said, "One that fits." If I asked oven temperature, she said, "Cake temperature." When I asked how long it should be in the oven, she said, "Until it's done." And so it went. Sensing my frustration with these answers, she would say, "Tracey, just use your mind. You do have a mind, don't you?" Then, she would launch into her story about the poor soul, back home, who lost her mind. Now, it is important to remember, I was fifteen at the time. My total knowledge, of any subject, was slim at best, and my patience was less than that. Needless to say, this period didn't do much for my cooking abilities, but ... I received many lessons in tolerance.

After I left Grandma, I turned to cookbooks. Contrary to Grandma's opinion, I never did need to know how to pluck a chicken. However, twenty years later, I was in Bermuda and definitely in need of Grandma's wisdom. I had left the mountains and my controlled environment with non-existent humidity. I was not familiar with the tools of the trade I found in my new home. I burned everything. Everything cooked too fast. My cakes fell, whipped cream didn't whip, my meringue turned to rain drops. After two decades of meal preparation, I had no idea what I was doing. Then, Grandma's words came back to me.

"Tracey, you're a woman, so you'll always be a cook. What you don't know is where this world will take you. I have cooked on mountains, in the prairies, at sea level, on ships, in bombed-out kitchens. I have cooked with no oven or stove. Even when I was supplied with an oven, often, I couldn't understand the controls. Some read Gas Mark 5; some were graded in Celsius temperatures; some had instructions in a foreign language. It all comes down to this: the only way you can cook is by using your senses and your mind. If your batter is too thin, add flour. If it's too thick, add water. When it pulls away from the side of the pan, or when you can smell it, it's done. Use your mind, Tracey. God gave you your eyes, nose, fingers and taste buds. Use them."

Grandma's prediction came true. Here I was, in another place, completely out of my element. Now, I had no choice. I had to take her advice.

Sea level temperature is *hotter*. Foods cook faster. Lower your temperature by at least twenty-five degrees and keep a close watch. Most likely, it will be done before it is "supposed" to be. On humid days, try not to make cakes, meringue or whipped cream. And ... this is very important – especially in the summer – get food to the fridge as quickly as possible. Remember, heat and humidity encourages things to grow, bad things, things you should not eat. Remember my advice: keep it clean, keep it dry, keep it moving? Now you can add keep it cold.

CHAPTER FIVE

The Isles of Rest?

CHRISTMAS

It was a wonderful evening. I had invited our favourite couple over for a tree-trimming party. Freshly baked goodies, nachos and a spicy meat dip, hot chocolate laced with Frangelico® and a host of other forbidden, fat-laden goodies tempted our taste buds while we listened to Christmas carols and decorated the tree. I had dutifully bought the popcorn, cranberries and candy canes. I popped the corn and froze the cranberries. We, the girls, strung popcorn and cranberries into garlands while the fellows put the lights on the tree. I wanted this to be an old-fashioned Christmas, just like home. Things were shaping up just fine. We all stood back and admired our work before saying good night to our friends and retiring, full and happy.

The following week, I noticed the tree was moving. I dismissed this thought, admonishing myself for having attended too many Christmas parties. When grey blobs began forming, I took a closer look. The popcorn had turned to mush. The cranberries had gone mouldy. The candy canes were providing Christmas treats for an army of 48,000 ants. Yes, the tree was moving, or rather, the ants were.

By this time I had been living in Bermuda for two years. I should have known better. Well ... life is learning experience. Consider yourself taught – do not put food, of any sort, on your Christmas tree.

This is but one of my Bermuda Christmas memories. There was the year Cassy told me I was not permitted to sing Christmas carols (apparently I'm not a great singer!). Then, there was the year a strange, injured chicken showed up at my door and spent the entire season in a laundry basket on the stereo. Ten days of round-the-clock Christmas carols was more than SHE bargained for!

Yes, I do miss the snow at Christmas, but there's a lot to be said for strolling along the beach on December 25.

EASTER

It was a week before Easter. After a few years of gentle nudging from my crew, I decided this was the year to take up the challenge, to "get with it" was the way they put it. Off I went – all I really needed was yeast. Now, you would think, after countless generations of celebrating Easter with traditional Easter treats, the grocery stores would know enough to stock ample supplies of Easter treat ingredients. Nope. A week before Easter, that year, not a packet of yeast was to be found on this island. Yeast is a tricky staple; it has a limited shelf life; it cannot be bought too far ahead. And, to my knowledge, there is no substitute. Again, planning is key.

There were no hot cross buns that year. But, I got it together the following Easter; I bought my yeast a month in advance. The buns turned out great.

Along with the buns, the traditional Easter brunch must include fish cakes. Paul's mother always ensured we were following custom by dropping in with her own homemade fish cakes and a dozen store-bought buns. This year I thought I would really surprise her by delivering my own homemade buns to her. As I walked up to her door, so did someone else, with a dozen hot cross buns – homemade! As I entered the living room, another dozen lay on the coffee table. As I put mine in the kitchen, I saw another dozen! Lordy, no wonder she never made them! Well, it's the thought that counts and she accepted them graciously – all of them.

HOLIDAYS

Many of Bermuda's special days are celebrated in much the same way as in Canada. However, on the island, Christmas includes cassava pie; Easter brings fish cakes, hot cross buns and kite flying. Look to the skies on Good Friday. Hundreds of homemade and store-bought kites flutter in the breezes as far as the eye can see. Some have hummers, noisemaking additions that do just that – hum. Horseshoe Bay and the larger public parks are certainly worth a visit on Good Friday.

Thanksgiving is not a holiday here, but many of the restaurants serve the traditional feast for the benefit of American tourists and residents. This happens in November for the American holiday. Canadian Thanksgiving, celebrated in October, seems to slip by me unnoticed. It's terrible, I know, but it's true. I'm busy with my volunteer work then – that's my excuse.

Cup Match is a major event. This two-day celebration revolves around a cricket game, played on the last Thursday and Friday of July or the first Thursday and Friday of August. A country fair atmosphere prevails. Amusement stalls, games of chance, fast food and Bermudian specialties are available for the spectators and those who simply want to take in the spirit of the event, see and be seen. Colourful new wardrobe selections, purchased at the many Cup Match sales, are evident. For those who normally would not work weekends, this holiday allows time for a four-day camping break or off-island excursion. Everyone, cricket lover or not, looks forward to Cup Match.

The Annual Exhibition, held in April, is well worth a visit. The Botanical Gardens, a showpiece in itself, serves as home for this annual three-day extravaganza. Displays, both amateur and professional, showcase the many varied talents of our island residents. Fruits and vegetables, baked goods, exotic creations and foods of all kinds are presented and judged in many different categories. Flowers, including roses, orchids and African violets, are displayed in all their glory. This is a great opportunity to see beautiful furniture and sculptures made from the famous Bermuda cedar tree, as well as a selection of Bermuda kites. Entries in the livestock competition (poultry, rabbits, pigs etc.) vie for winning ribbons. Lectures and demonstrations take place inside while marching bands, tugs-of-war, gymnasts and all manner of horse competitions entertain those outside. There's something for everyone here.

Bermuda Day, May 24, is celebrated with a bicycle race, a half marathon (13 miles), a fitted dinghy race, a parade and a fair at the National Sports Centre.

Spring (mid April through May) is a great time to go open housing. On Wednesday afternoons, the Garden Club of Bermuda sponsors the opening of some of Bermuda's most interesting homes to visitors. One ticket gains entrance to several homes, carefully chosen to be within a short distance of each other. Ticket proceeds provide scholarship assistance for horticulturally inclined students. Also on display are gorgeous flower arrangements created by the club members. This is a great way to get decorating ideas for your Bermuda home. Tourists love this excursion, so will you.

The various schools and some charitable organizations hold fairs throughout the year. Mount Saint Agnes', in October, is the largest. Watch the papers, drop in, see what's going on and support these events. If you have the time, offer your help. I've had piles of fun work-

71

ing in the bake stalls selling Portuguese donuts faster than the speed of light! I've also contributed all sorts of baking. On one occasion, Dad (who was visiting at the time) followed me and my Bermuda rum cake to the bake stall, bought *my* cake and brought it right back home again!

ENTERTAINMENT

The plane was landing in five minutes. The stranger, sitting in the window seat, tapped my shoulder and said, "Why is the water so clear?"

Many books about Bermuda are available – read them – get to know the island, learn the basics. Every visitor you meet will ask you a dozen questions, like the one above. This is an experience somewhat reminiscent of parenting a three-year-old. The questions never stop. Why is the sky blue? Why is water wet? Family, friends and tourists will inundate you with queries. After the sixth "I don't know" response, one begins to feel a little foolish. Try to keep yourself out of this state, do your homework. The water is clear because instead of brown dirt on the bottom, we have white sand AND because ocean water in this neck of the woods contains very few nutrients. Why? I don't know. ~

The cultural event of the year is the Bermuda Festival. Every January and February world-renowned artists converge on the island to perform every manner of entertainment to sold-out shows. Get your tickets early; they're available in October.

Theatre productions are happening all the time. Read the newspapers, it's all there. If you're accustomed to large city papers, you'll find Bermuda's are a breeze. You can read cover to cover in an hour – there's no reason to miss a thing.

Bermuda has four movie theatres showing current movies at roughly the same cost and at roughly the same release times as those in Canada and the States. Because this is a popular form of entertainment here, it is wise to purchase your tickets ahead of time for the two Hamilton theatres. I haven't heard of any sold-out problems for the theatres in Somerset and St. George's.

Videos are also available here, even at some gas stations! The library has a video section as well. I strongly recommend that you get a library membership.

Hamilton has several nightclubs. If you engage in this type of activity often, it would be wise to get a membership – most have a cover charge. Pubs are everywhere, many with entertainment.

The large hotels, in prime season, have live entertainment. At some, dinner is included. Dinner is also included in cruises around the harbour.

Until you get into the swing of things, always call first. This includes restaurants. Hours change with the seasons, when the owners are away, for funerals, for lunch and a dozen other reasons. While you have them on the phone, also check dress restrictions. Smart casual means *no* T-shirts, track shoes or jeans.

TRAVEL

At "home" it's called Cabin Fever.

Once you have moved here, travel will inevitably become part of your life. This is just as well; it's important to get away. Three trips a year will negate any "rock fever" symptoms. Also, a return to the concrete jungle, the rat race, the snow, ice and cold, will increase your appreciation of the island. Tourists often ask me if I feel like I'm going to fall into the ocean or if I worry about a very big wave washing me away. No, never. However, I do occasionally experience a low energy, no motivation, ho-hum state of mind. A trip cures this. It doesn't need to be a long trip and the destination doesn't matter. My research on this subject has concluded that three is the number to aim for. Any more and life becomes chaotic. Any less and the "fever" sets in. A change is as good as a rest, I suppose.

Travel brings up customs – customs' duty that is. For any trip over 72 hours you are entitled to a duty-free allowance. This amount can change with the yearly government budget, but, whatever the amount, it's never enough. If you're honest, it's difficult to stay under this allowance. Human nature pressures us to "get away with it", by not claiming several articles in order to stay under our allowance and avoid paying duty. My personal feelings: I live in a country without income tax and reap the benefits of this. I travel on the roads; I relax on the beaches; I admire the flowers in the roundabout. SOMEONE has to pay for this. In large part, this money comes from customs duties. It is not mandatory that I buy that last item that pushes me over my limit, any more than it's mandatory that I pick up a bag of trash on Keep Bermuda Beautiful days. This is a choice I make. It's a type of donation. Also, I don't have a good enough memory to be a successful liar. Remembering just what I did buy and which of that I did claim and what story I will tell if questioned is just too darn complicated. For these reasons, I claim what I buy and let the customs officer sort it out. If these items were not a great buy, I wouldn't have them in the first place. Peace of mind is worth the few extra dollars.

However, my acquisition of gifts by mail is another story. All incoming parcels must be opened and examined by a postal clerk at the Post Office. If the contents are valued over the $20 gift limit, duty must be paid. I do not want to open my CHRISTMAS gift December 3rd in the POST OFFICE! I do not want to try to establish the true value of this merchandise and I CERTAINLY do not want to pay duty on those items I neither want nor need! But, this is the law of the land; I must abide by it or find a way to negate it. I did. Long ago, I instructed my family and friends NOT to send any more gifts by mail. For the most part, this ended these exercises in frustration.

I deal with gifts when I travel. When I go home I take the belated (or early) birthday and Christmas gifts with me. I think it's a great system. I can pick up suitable items whenever the mood strikes me; I can shop for good buys, here and away; gifts arrive with me, under no time restrictions or postage costs. (My aunt once sent me a sweater vest valued at $15. The postage was $8.78. What's wrong with this picture?)

HOUSESITTING

June 26, 1992

One of my pals called this morning. She has just arrived back from a two-week trip. She's not happy. In her absence, her home went mouldy. It's everywhere she says – on the clothes, the walls, the tiles, the floors, the toilet. I know for a fact this lady maintains a clean home. But, unfortunately, it has rained the entire time she has been away. It's been humid. Nothing in her home was kept dry. Nothing was kept moving. As I explained to her, she should have had a housesitter.

This housesitting business was a new phenomenon for me. It's a big deal here. Most people I know have housesitters. So do I. It's a mutually beneficial arrangement: the sitter gets free alternative lodging, the owner gets peace of mind. Policemen and nurses are popular choices. Often you will see ads in the newspaper placed by couples who wish to housesit. Many couples from abroad wish to visit their working children in Bermuda. Most "working children" live in small studio apartments not conducive to company, and hotel rates can be prohibitive to pensioners.

There are excellent reasons to bring someone in. A "lived-in" appearance tends to keep potential thieves at bay. Any emergency can be dealt with immediately. (In two hours, a broken pipe under my kitchen sink flooded three rooms – imagine if this had been a two-week absence!) A summer hurricane is a possibility. Pets and plants will be attended to. Very high on the list is this mildew problem. Without even trying, housesitters will keep things moving and keep things dry. They will open and close doors; they will flush the toilet and run water; they will close curtains and open windows. A good housesitter will also keep things clean. And that's the solution to my pal's dilemma. Keep things moving, keep them dry and keep them clean. You must have this memorized by now, right?

Pay them? Well ... this is an individual choice. There are no written housesitting rules. I do not know anyone who pays for this service – as I said, it's mutually beneficial. However, I do know of some who bring souvenirs of their trip home to their sitter. I don't do this because: a tiny apartment has no room for "my" ornaments; this person is probably pinching pennies and would rather have the ten bucks; it's a hassle (shopping, packing, customs); and most importantly, does your sitter REALLY want ... a Jamaican fertility goddess?

BEACHES

"Look at those crazy people in the water. It's December for heaven's sake!" This oft-heard exclamation is explained away by the next one, "They must be Canadians!"

I find it amazing that people are lumped together like this. From the time we are old enough to listen we are told, "Everyone is different ... each person is an individual ... there will always be those greater and lesser than yourself" and so on. Yet, somehow, nationalities pick up their very own sticker: Canadians are cheap, Americans are aggressive, Germans are efficient, the English are stuffy, Italians are hot-tempered. In the case of the crazy Canadians in the water, I can only surmise that this label follows the news we get about that country: "There's a cold front coming down from Canada". It's no wonder that half the world thinks Canadians live in igloos and eat polar bears! But, I must admit, most ocean-swimmers in December ARE Canadians!

Traditionally, Bermudians enjoy the ocean from May 24 to September 1. This is when the water is the warmest – within a few degrees of the air temperature. But, try telling a Canadian that a 70 degree ocean is cold! Or, for that matter, that a 65 degree winter day is "freezing." Canadian cold is measured in minus degrees – below zero. If you're looking to meet a few fellow Canadians, try the beaches, anytime. Even October to May ... they'll be there.

Bermuda's most famous beach is Horseshoe Bay on the South Shore. This is the beach to see and on which to be seen. It's big, beautiful and popular. All the amenities are there: food, drinks, showers, washrooms. If this is not your cup of tea, there are dozens of others to choose from. Some are very private; some are good for snorkelling; some are good for children and some are good for the adventurous. Whoever you are and whatever you like, there's a beach for you. Try them all, find your own favorite.

Now for the cautions (as always). Nothing's perfect.

Avoiding the beaches between the hours of 11 a.m. and 2 p.m. is sound advice. This is the period the beaches are busiest and the sun is deadliest. In summer, it's hot round-the-clock so this is not a problem. Remember your sunscreen! Surely, you've heard enough about this. Sun poisoning is a real threat for the concrete jungle dwellers. Despite my warnings, several of our guests have spent agonizing nights, lobster-red and ill.

Because the islands of Bermuda are surrounded by reefs, strange and dangerous creatures of the deep are seldom found close to shore. One exception to this is a jellyfish-like organism called the Portuguese man-of-war. As it floats on the water's surface, strong storm waves can wash it over the reefs and onto the shore. If you see what appears to be a bluish purple bubble, the size of a mouse, stay away. Extending from this bubble are threads or strings (tiny tentacles) containing a burning "acid." This substance produces a painful, red welt upon contact. Scott was stung once. This guy is the epitome of tough and brave, but tears ran down his face for 24 hours. Watching this nearly killed ME! It's unlikely you will ever get wound up with one of these little devils. I don't want to scare you away from wonderful beach days. Just be aware and watch your little children – they would think this purple bubble was just the neatest thing, sitting there on the beach!

If you or yours should fall victim to this little creature, remember, the "threads" stick on contact. Remove them immediately with anything but your fingers! Vinegar, meat tenderizer or pawpaw juice will reduce the pain. Larger jellyfish such as those found in Mexican waters can cause severe shock symptoms. This seldom happens here, but watch for the signs. The welts will heal on their own in a few days.

Now don't screw up your nose at this but I must tell you, there is tar on the beaches. We have passing ships to thank for this. You may never see it but there's every likelihood that you will come home with a bit on your feet or shoes or swimsuit or towel. Products containing petroleum distillates remove tar effectively. I use Lestoil™. Baby oil or salad oil works well too. Be sure and check your feet after each beach day or it will also be all over your rugs – a real nuisance!

Just before I leave this topic, let me mention something I've just learned. It is almost impossible to make a white material that is not see-through when wet. Guess who just bought a white swimsuit? Guess who just read an article explaining the reasons *not* to buy a white swimsuit? Guess who ran to check the transparency of her new purchase? Me, me and me. I thought carefully about this choice of color. I reasoned that if I chose white, the sun wouldn't fade it and the chlorine in pools wouldn't bleach it out. Well, that may all be true but I STILL need a new swimsuit, in any color but white. Sheesh. I can't win. But, I do try. Another day, another lesson learned. This is why we should live two lifetimes. It takes seventy-five *years* to learn all this stuff! Then, possessed with all this wisdom, we die. Now, what kind of sense does that make?

CHAPTER SIX

Wheels Within Wheels

BIKES

"It is very important," he said, "to keep your bike speed under 50 kph." I had obviously missed something ... again. Why would this be a problem? I had never biked at anything close to that speed in my life!

The term *bike* will throw you off but just for a very short while. Here, a bike is a motor-assisted cycle, a moped, a motorcycle. A bike, as I had always known it, is referred to as a pedal cycle. As in other parts of the world, young Bermudians clock many miles on these – their first experience on wheels. However, with the spread-out nature of the island and the distinct possibility that friends will be scattered in every parish, these youngsters become road-wise early and quickly. Within a year of our move here, my 12-year-old son had developed legs of steel. By the age of 15, a normal Sunday ride was from one end of the island to the other and, I might add, the ingestion of enough food to feed the Regiment in order to replace the calories this exercise required! While he was certainly at one with his pedal cycle, still, he couldn't wait to "be legal".

This term refers to the right, at age 16, to own and ride a 50 cc moped – a bike. There is no question as to what the birthday gift for a 16-year-old will be. This marks a major milestone, a coming-out, an opening of the cage and yes, Mom, they will take advantage and get cocky and speed. Then, they will be caught. They may lose their licence ... but usually only once. Witnessing true misery is watching a legal teen survive his "off-the-road" time.

Legal teens are only a portion of Bermuda's bike world. At age 18, a rider may upgrade to an 80 cc or up to the maximum 150 cc bike. This is as much power as one would ever need for these roads. Many businessmen, my husband included, prefer this mode of transport. The ease of parking in town and ability to scoot by most of the rush hour traffic make it an ideal choice. Bermuda law dictates one car per household; generally, Mom gets the car – she's in charge of the groceries. Seniors, too, appreciate this low cost, low maintenance, no hassle, efficient way of getting about. I still smile when I see helmeted 80-year-olds motoring down Front Street. I also smile when I see businessmen in shorts. Indoctrination takes a long, long time.

Okay, back to bikes. There are some important points to remember. Always, always wear a helmet. It's the law. Remember, if you leave your helmet with your bike, turn it top side up! Sudden showers happen often. Rain makes for slippery roads and the self-explanatory "road rash" – be careful. In a downpour, slip into a bus shelter, downpours usually last only a few minutes. As I mentioned in my "winter" spiel, get yourself some raingear (rubberized pants and jacket, gum boots). In summer, a bike ride is cool and refreshing; in winter it can be darn cold. Bring your scarf and gloves. Keep a brown paper grocery bag in your winter kit. Place it under your jacket and over your chest – very effective in cutting the cold wind. Your rain jacket will also keep the wind at bay. Be wary of summer touring and "moped thighs". Bike-induced breezes will keep you cool, but the tops of your legs will scream "SUNBURN" that night.

The speed limit is not 50 kph, it's really 35 kph or 20 miles per hour but, as long as you keep your vehicle under 50 kph, you'll be travelling at the same speed as everyone else. If you should notice five cars piled up behind you, pull over and let them pass safely.

I would probably have another page of biking suggestions for you, but I must admit that this is not the mode of transportation I use. My first three experiences with bikes were NOT fun. The first time, I dismounted on the wrong side and scorched my calf on the muffler. The next time, a red bee hit my husband's helmet, fell on the inside of my thigh and was just mad enough to get revenge on the most tender part of my anatomy! Still, never-say-die Tracey figured she should learn to operate one of these pain-inducing machines. My daughter gave me lessons. She neglected, however, to tell me she had a brake problem. There were none! I didn't hit the German Shepherd dog in my path, but I did come within two feet of plunging over the Astwood Cove cliff. After that, I sort of lost interest.

Be that as it may, I highly recommend bike transport. In place of a car, it will do wonders for your bank account. The three in my crew figure it's the cat's whiskers! Thousands of others agree!

NEW YEAR'S

New Year's Day 1990

I was standing in the kitchen, sleepily scooping coffee into the pot. I was thinking about the peaceful, relaxing day ahead. Nothing was planned. I didn't have to DO anything. I heard a small voice behind me. It was Scott. All he said was, "Mom?" I was immediately awake. That one word, spoken quietly, with just the hint of a quiver filled me with foreboding. I had heard it before.

The time he biked INTO a moving car, I heard it. The time he went tobogganing UNDER a moving car, I heard it. And the time he got wound up in barbed wire and the time he fell out of a tree and so on and so on. That quiver was my first clue that something was sorely amiss. I turned around to search his eyes for confirmation. It was there.

Slowly he turned so I could see his left side. All the skin, from his shoulder to his toes was gone. This raw, red mess was covered in gravel. I looked into his eyes and he said, "Last night was the worst night of my life." Tears streaming down my face, I ever so delicately tried to clean him up. I didn't do well; my hands were shaking.

While I waited for Paul to bring him home from the hospital, I relived the night before and my speech to him and Cassy: "If you're going to drink, don't come home. Stay where you are. Do not ride your bike. Take a taxi. Scott, why don't you go with Cassy, you can keep an eye on each other?" You know, the regular "Mom-type" speech. I was a little concerned about Scott that night because he was reeling with emotion over a recently lost love. Couple that with a night of New Year's celebrations – a sure recipe for trouble.

What went wrong? Cassy was home. HER skin was intact. She wandered out of her room at noon wondering what all the fuss was about. I couldn't explain it, I didn't know myself. When I showed her the beautiful three-piece suit Scott had proudly pranced in the night before, she pretty well figured it out. The left half was gone.

It was suppertime before I got the details. Scott was drinking but remembering my orders, he did not drive home. Instead, he let his friend borrow his bike to drive him home. So far so good? No. His friend was in the same state. How can a mother possibly cover all these bases?

Anyway, the bike went down and Scott took a long ride at ground level. He left his skin and his suit somewhere on Harvey Road. I'm not convinced that he's learned his lesson, but he has some pretty visible scars as reminders.

The moral of this story: Give your children this speech. Give yourself this speech and your husband. Include in addition: Don't let your drunk friend drive you home. Please, please remember, unlike a car driver, a bike rider is not encased in a metal capsule. Gravel, at 30 mph, is an exfoliator of the highest degree.

August 10, 1992: 2 a.m.

I'm sitting (in my underwear) relating the above story to you. The door opens and in walks Scott from another night on the town. He has two female tourists with him. They didn't have the taxi fare to Dockyard. The buses aren't running. This is life with Scott. Cassy (who is suspicious of the MAILMAN) never presents me with these dilemmas.

CARS

I staggered in the back door, saw my daughter in the kitchen and said, "I need a double vodka, quick!"

This was the scene immediately following my first driving lesson on Bermuda's roads. Four months later I got my licence; four months after that, I was still dealing with the jitters. It was time to get a grip. I set aside the month of February to accomplish this goal.

My plan of attack was this: each day it was mandatory that I get in the car and go somewhere, anywhere, even around the block. After 28 days of this, I would either be comfortable with these roads or awfully familiar with this block! This system did me a world of good, but it was another year before I was comfortable behind the steering wheel. Even now, I do not take my eyes off the road. (To all the acquaintances who wonder why I don't wave ... I don't even see you!)

Heaven only knows what's behind every bend in the road and there's a bend every 100 feet! I'm sure I've seen it all: horses, buggies, walkers, runners, geese, goats, even tourists – on the wrong side! Between this and driving on the left, I was an accident waiting to happen. I crawled around every curve chanting "left is right" as though it was a mantra. When my husband said, "Turn right," I did and entered the roundabout backwards. (This is the only time I have seen Paul on the edge of panic!) *Left is right.* What with the geese, the roundabouts and the left is right business (not to mention the Bermudian habit of honking at every known person), I was a nervous wreck. I gripped the steering wheel as if I was suspended over a precipice. I simply had to relax and get this behind me. I was not going to be held prisoner in my house by this fear. This was my free-

84

dom, my transportation. (I had still not made my peace with bikes.)

Controls, again with the controls: Bermuda's car laws are strict. Length, width, wheelbase and horsepower are restricted. With the exception of new cars, yearly vehicle examinations are mandatory. (New cars are exempt the first and third year.) Our car failed the first test. The inspector found a fingernail size dent in the rear. We failed the second year too. The very classy black border Paul placed around the licence plate was not acceptable. If you own a car, have any problems repaired BEFORE you have it tested. If you fail, you're "off the road". It's pretty difficult to get your car repaired when you can't drive it anywhere. Finally, allow yourself plenty of time for any business at Transport Control. Once you're established, you can use the mail-in option for licence renewal. Much better.

As with all things in Bermuda, keep your car clean. Between the humidity and the salt, rust is just a moment away. I also don't recommend leaving your car at the airport for extended trips. We did this once and it looked like a derelict on our return – a result of the wind and saltspray.

The purchase of a car is a personal decision. Gasoline, parts and sticker prices are high. However, a tank of gas goes a long way. (Where are you going to go?) If your contract is short, try to get away without this purchase. It's possible. You'll be many thousands of dollars ahead and that pays for a lot of taxis.

Oh yes, one more thing. When you take your computerized driver's test, be aware the word "curb" is spelled "kerb". That really threw me at the time.

BUSES & FERRIES

"I'm NOT going to the ends of the earth to travel with pigs and chickens!"

A great trivia question: Where is Bermuda located? (I would also be most interested in knowing, exactly, where the "ends of the earth" are.)

Bermuda is NOT a third world country; farm animals do NOT travel on public transportation. Furthermore, Bermuda is NOT: at the ends of the earth, in the Caribbean, or even close to all those other countries that begin with a "B" (Barbuda, Bahamas, Belgium). We have one of the highest standards of living in the world AND we are one THOUSAND miles north of the Caribbean. This I pointed out to Bob, the caller above.

It was important to Cassy that Bob attend her high school graduation. Obviously, Bob had never been here before. Now, how do I put this delicately? Well, Bob lives his life ... in comfort. He drives an assortment of vehicles but his favourite is his Lincoln. When he found out he wouldn't be able to rent a CAR, much less a Lincoln, he had a fit. I suggested the bus. The above was his response. Sigh.

As I explained to Bob, Bermuda has an excellent bus and ferry system. Bus tickets, sold in sheets of 15, are less than half the cost of cash fare. You really don't want to mess around with this cash fare business. It must be exact, in coin, and is expensive. Better value yet are the passes. These are available for one and three days, a week, a month and three months (great for the school term if you have kids). This same pass can be used on the ferry as well.

The island is divided into 14 zones, each about two miles long and buses run end to end. Stops are marked with pink or blue poles. Pink designates buses going INTO the City of Hamilton. Blue means they are going AWAY FROM the city.

Ferries provide relaxing, picturesque travel. Beautiful homes, not visible from the road, can be appreciated in this way. Many business professionals choose this mode of daily transport to avoid rush hour traffic and parking problems. While animals are not permitted (Bob!), for an extra charge, bikes may be taken on the Dockyard route.

Now and then I take the bus to town just for the heck of it. It's a pleasant change watching the scenery instead of the road, not worrying about parking, mingling with the tourists and locals. I suggest you take a few bus rides. Take a map and follow it along. Without even trying, you'll learn a lot.

Ferries are another pleasant way to spend the day. Take a bus to town, take the ferry to Somerset or Dockyard, have a good walkabout, ferry back to town and bus it home. This is also an interesting, inexpensive excursion for visitors from away.

You can only appreciate the incredible beauty of this country if you get out and see it. Bermuda is much more than the City of Hamilton. Don't worry if you get lost – anyone you see will be happy to sort you out. This includes you, FELLOWS, bite the bullet – ask directions!

We were successful in getting Bob to Bermuda. He rented a bike. He was happy as a clam.

CHAPTER SEVEN

The Good.
The Bad. The Ugly.

CATS & RATS

"Holy smokes! Holy smokes! Mumble. Grumble. Holy smokes. HOLY SMOKES!"

My husband spews forth this unintelligible dissertation on a regular basis. Over time, I have learned to translate. This spiel means, "Tracey, there is a major problem here. I can't deal with it. DO SOMETHING!" More often than not, it concerns an animal – alive, dead or in-between.

In the wild mammal line, cats and rats predominate. Fortunately, the former prey on the latter – an effective means of control. I have no fear of either. Rats have only caused me two problems: burying the victims who had the audacity to wander into our cats' domain and the decision to be made upon the discovery of one not quite ready for burial. If you find yourself with a rat problem, adopt a cat. Alternatively, call the Health Department. They will set traps, remove the contents and solve this problem for you.

On the other hand, cats have caused me no end of heartache. To see a skinny, dirty, starving little creature with its nose pressed against my screen door is more than I can bear. Ultimately, over the years, this resulted in the adoption of dozens of cats and the wrenching job of having half of them put down. Do not, I repeat, do not feed these little waifs or you are destined to the same fate. You must resist the innate female inclination to nurture, love and protect every small, helpless, injured living thing. These cats are wild or, worse, abandoned. One third of them have "Cat AIDS", no threat to human beings but with the same prognosis as human AIDS and the possibility of infecting other cats. This was the story of Midnight, a jet-black male.

He appeared one day and never left. He stole Cassy's heart. When it became apparent that I couldn't separate the two, we made a deal – she would pay the vet bill to have him "checked out". If all tests came back negative, we would adopt him. If they didn't, she would be responsible for the medical bills to get him healthy. I thought I had all bases covered and resigned myself to the fact that, either way, we would be adopting our third cat. The result of the tests was my introduction to this killer disease. He tested positive. What a dilemma! Cassy was away – I had to sort this out before her return. I wrestled with it for two days. I phoned her. Then, Scott, Midnight and I drove to vet. It was Midnight's last trip. I cried for two days.

White cats are particularly prone to skin cancer, especially of the ears. And this was the fate of Angel. She appeared early one morning, nose pressed against the back door screen. As I crawled out of the stupor called sleep, I heard the "Holy Smokes" speech. Now what? "The back door, do something," was the reply. This was the saddest sight I'd ever seen. Only half-grown and pure white, this little critter had a head covered in tumors. She was starving, dirty. She was tame. I went out and sat on the grass. She climbed into my lap, looked straight into my eyes and cried. I went to pieces.

That was Saturday. I couldn't see the vet till Monday. In this short space of time, she worked her magic on us all. I had never seen such a cat, so loving, so attentive. She looked deep into my eyes and talked to me constantly. I fed her, I bathed her, I brushed her. She loved it all – she was an absolute angel.

By Monday, there was no question. We would do whatever we had to, to get her well. Off I went to the vet.

I left there alone, devastated. She had inoperable, incurable, rampant cancer. The vet wouldn't even DISCUSS an alternative; she had to be put down. I was a long time getting over Angel. I'm crying now.

I learned my lesson. When I found three starving kittens in the middle of the road, I took them to the SPCA. (*But*, I must admit, *not until* I brought them home, cleaned them up, fed them, put them in a basket, took a picture and assured myself that they had, in their short little lives, been allowed one day of tender loving care.) I didn't call back. If they had not been adopted, I didn't want to know.

Presently, we have four cats. Our maximum is three, but there you have it. Generally, a wild cat has half the life span of a domestic so the situation tends to resolve itself. These four seem to be a particularly strong bunch, probably because they have the genes of Hercules. As the name implies, Herc is the toughest son of a gun in the valley. He is the only cat I have ever feared. Even the vet will only see him after he's been tranquilized. He arrived in a dreadful state (don't they all?) and, at that time, was estimated to be eleven years old. That was six years ago and he's still the only one of the four that climbs trees, runs across the roof and is in a steady state of motion. Due to Herc's temperament, I knew from the beginning that he couldn't be an adoptee. *We* know how to handle him; *we* know *he's* the boss; we know, *you don't mess with Herc*. So, we have him for life. Because of Herc, we also have Mr. Grey for life.

Mr. Grey lived under the car for six months. He was the most spooked cat I've ever known. Even after three years with us, he's still spooked. Herc is his hero; Mr. Grey positively worships Herc. He follows him everywhere, does what he does and wails like a Siamese when Herc is out of his line of vision. I think of him as a teenager – completely messed up. So, between his skittish character and this hero worship and the depression that's going to set in when Herc passes on, it just wouldn't be fair to place him in a new home. Cheeky, on the other hand, is ready for adoption.

Cheeky arrived when we were away. He just marched in the back door and took over. Our housesitter gave him his name. We think he was abandoned because he tamed in two weeks and has been an absolute treasure ever since. All he wants is to be brushed and loved, day and night. He's a pretty cat with a gentle personality and never, ever gets into any trouble. Tuxedo, on the other hand, is a pain in the neck.

Tux is absolutely gorgeous and an absolute brat. He unrolls the paper towels and then shreds them; he empties the Tupperware™ cupboard; he pulls all the cat food cans onto the counter which then roll onto the floor, he's trouble incarnate. Being nocturnal, he starts all this foolishness at midnight whereupon it sounds like the Russian army is coming through the kitchen. Despite this, he is the one everyone wants – he has the looks, the character, the personality. You might wonder why we still have him. Well, let me tell you *that* story

I found a lovely lady who fell in love with Tux. Late at night, we took him to his new location in a sealed box, in the car. We stayed there with him and had tea while he checked out his new home. The next morning this lady called me. She was in quite a state. Tux had escaped in the night. Both she and I searched the neighbourhood – no luck. While I was concerned, I knew Tux. His intelligence, his daring, his charm would pull him through. He would survive. Some kind-hearted soul would feed him and fall in love with him and he would be fine. Six days later, Paul called me into the yard. There, walking up the driveway, just as happy as a clam, was Tux. He had walked from Somerset to Warwick, a distance of six miles, in six days. Heaven only knows the adventures he encountered crossing golf courses, roads, bridges, private property – who knows what? And what inner intelligence led the way? I would really like to know this. In any case, I know he would do it again. I won't risk it. Tux the Trekker will also be with us for life.

You can see the complications that arise in my mission. Until I find the ones I have new homes, I can't provide a foster home, taming, medical care, food and attention to the ones, sick and starving, still roaming out there. The only way to end this cycle of misery is to stop the kittens from coming along in the first place. Neutering is encouraged by both the Government and SPCA. One would think, on an island this size, that every animal could find a home. Nope, not yet. But, it's coming.

In 1992, a group of volunteers established the Bermuda Feline Assistance Bureau (BFAB). Their mission: to control Bermuda's wild cat population by neutering and spaying. To this end, they supply traps, deliver the animal to a vet, have it spayed or neutered and return it to its territory. Dozens of cat colonies have also been set up where *hundreds* of cats are cared for daily. Only animals with fatal diseases are put down; they do not support euthanasia. Six hundred cats per year are dealt with in this way, resulting in *tens of thousands* of kittens *not* being born. If you have a wild cat problem, give them a call; if you have time or money to spare, donate!

If one of these orphans should steal your heart, make a commitment for life, or not at all. Have it checked, bathed and vaccinated by the vet immediately. And please, please, please, please, have it neutered. Bermuda has so, so many suffering animals without homes, do your bit to put an end to this.

DOGS & TOADS

Dogs and toads – a likely combination!

I write about these two together because they share one amazing trait. Both have the ability to instil fear in the general Bermudian population. I am constantly reminded and confounded by this. I grew up with both in my country but so did they. Much thought on this subject has come to nought. I can't figure it out. But then, I don't understand a fear of thunder or lightning or hurricanes either. On the other hand, why something as small and harmless as a cockroach causes terror in my soul is also a mystery to me. Fear is a strange and personal thing.

Many residents have dogs. This seems to be more for the perceived protection factor than the desire for a pet. I suppose if I had grown up thinking a dog's only purpose was to guard house and home, I too would be wary. Apparently, long before my time, packs of wild dogs roamed the island. This, no doubt, also had an effect on the psyche of Bermudians.

All the fuss over dogs has, over the years, led to a strict set of controls. Yes, you may bring your dog to Bermuda but, first, you must complete the required paperwork and examinations. Get onto this early! There are no quarantine facilities on the island. If your pet arrives without proper documentation, back he goes. This happens. Once here, the dog MUST be licensed. Neutered animals have a reduced fee. You must not let them roam. No matter how docile your pet, do not allow it to "terrorize" the locals. It will. Keep it on a leash. If you are expecting a visitor to your property, keep the dog inside. November to March is the only time dogs are allowed on the beach – on a leash. Basically, keep in mind the fear I have mentioned – be considerate – keep your dog to yourself.

I love dogs. Try as he might, Paul has had limited success in his efforts to instill a "healthy" fear in me. It's just not there. I'm certain this is why I have never had a problem with dogs in the first place. Their instincts are far sharper than ours; they immediately go on alert when faced with a panic-stricken person. This sets the stage for trouble.

One of our neighbours has a dog. I don't know the neighbour but I do know the dog. Every once in a while I climb the back cliff to break the monotony of his day. He howls, and I mean HOWLS, all day long. It's the saddest song; I feel sorry for him..I'm sure his owners work; he's left alone all day, every day. He's lonely and bored. My trips up the cliff give him a chance to put on a mean face, bark, jump, growl and carry-on – defending his territory. It breaks up his day, gives him something else to think about and proves his worth: another day, another invasion thwarted! I've thought about calling his owners to set up a schedule whereby I would take him for a walk each day. It would be good for him, it would be good for me. It would be good for you! If dog walking, or, for that matter, cat petting, appeals to you, call the SPCA. They are always looking for help such as this.

As for toads: they're big, they're brown, they're ugly. You will only see them at night and after rain in the summer. They were introduced to Bermuda from Guyana in 1875 as a biological control for cockroaches and any creature that eats roaches is a friend of mine! The locals tell me that they spit poison but this is an embellishment. Actually, when attacked, glands located on their back secrete a substance poisonous to dogs. This could pose a serious problem for a small curious dog. This poison can kill. Convulsions may be your first clue (rinse his mouth thoroughly with vinegar and get to the vet). Don't panic about this possibility. I, personally, do not know anyone who has faced this situation. It would seem sensible, though, to keep your dog inside on rainy summer nights if he is the small curious type. As far as I can determine, this poison only affects dogs, not people or other animals. Strange.

ARCHIE

He was my favourite. He had never been allowed to be part of the group – always banished to the perimeter of the action. As the locals say, "He took some licks." His life had been such a tough one; I had to try and make him feel special. I did. I protected him. This time though, his foe was lethal. Although I thwarted the attacker, I was too late. He took two steps toward me and then ... he died.

This is the story of Archie, a beautiful, white, young Bantam rooster. He could fly over the house. This performance always impressed me. I could hear him – he sounded like a helicopter, and I would run outside to watch. If I stroked his beak, he would go into a trance. Really. He fascinated me. His last moments were spent trying to take to the skies, but the dog was too quick. I cried a lot that day.

Archie was one of the original five chickens that wandered into our yard one day and decided to stay. I kept waiting for a farmer to come and claim them. It didn't happen. I knew absolutely nothing about LIVE poultry and had NO intention of learning. Three months later, ten little black chicks buried my resolve. That began my four-year fascination with "wild" chickens.

This period of my life is a book in itself. I will try to be brief. Each of these chickens had a name, a personality and a set place in the pecking order. As I watched them, I became more and more engrossed. I tried to find some information (oh no, not more research!). All I could discover about these creatures was the result of caging, manipulation, selective breeding – man's interference. I stopped reading and began watching. It wasn't long before I confidently felt I had become the Jane Goodall of chickens. Seriously! The more I saw, the more impressed I became. Lessons of life, of motherhood, of machismo, of protection

94

and survival, of birth and death – it was all there. I have always worshipped Mother Nature, but this experience simply blew me away. They had a crystal ball. The day before the hurricane, the chickens KNEW. The day before the earthquake, the chickens KNEW. Every detail to ensure survival was in place with absolutely no help from me – the one with the brain. Their water bowl was an upturned leaf which caught the rain; their food was the seeds and bugs and plants growing profusely in my yard; their bed was the trees. Their bath was the dirt; their raincoats, oil produced by a gland under the tail. With their beaks they spread this oil all over their feathers each night before retiring. They had a language to signal the discovery of a food source, alarm, comfort, distress, aggravation and frustration. I learned this language. We're talking here of many, many, many hours of observation.

As time went by, more chicks came along and were occasionally orphaned. I taught them to fly. I taught them which plants they could eat. I became a surrogate hen. Talk about being needed! Talk about being wanted! We had to start eating the eggs – things were getting out of hand. Now these were eggs – fresh, fresh, fresh with bright orange yolks – and we had plenty of them. I didn't have a problem eating these eggs, but the moment the hen decided to sit, I wouldn't touch her eggs. My hens taught me a lot about how I really feel about abortion – and five hundred other puzzling "ethical" issues. They also gave me many hours of entertainment.

Do not believe chickens are stupid. This is a fallacy. My chickens pecked at the back door when they wanted to see me. They flew to my shoulder when I hung out the wash; they sat on my lap and went to sleep every time I got down to their level. One day they found me lying on the driveway and raised such a fuss, I had to get up! I'm sure they thought I was dead. If I went out to sit with them and wore earrings or sunglasses or shoes, they pecked them until I took them off – that was not the me they knew. When I called, they came. The roosters brought me bugs (I tried to be appreciative). I could go on and on about my life with the chickens – many stories here.

Four years after my love affair with these critters began, I had to make a decision. Life was becoming very complicated. Family matters meant I was travelling more, much more. Each time, I returned home to find another two dozen chicks. Our tourist cottage had become a hit. These guests were not impressed with the daily 5 a.m. wake-up call of three roosters ... five roosters ... nine roosters. There were things I wanted to do with my life, but these animals had a way of consuming all my free time. I had developed allergies; I suspected them. I made the decision. I gave them away. I have not regretted that decision, but I would not want to relive that day. Years have passed. I still miss them and wish I could have both worlds.

Now, I'm sure you are wondering what on earth all this has to do with moving to Bermuda. Three things. Number one: to impress upon you again the dangers of adopting anything that appears at your back door. Number two: to point out that you just never know what may come along to fill all those lonely hours you may think you'll have. Number three: it's a neat story.

By the way, my allergies were not caused by the chickens.

BIRDS

One evening in 1951, David Wingate, a Bermudian naturalist, witnessed an astonishing discovery. A musky smell and footprints led to the nest of a bird. This bird was the cahow, believed extinct for over three hundred years!

Along with the reefs, the cahow hindered the settlement of Bermuda until the early 1600's. Loud cries (sounding like "tell'em, tell'em") from thousands of these creatures pierced the night's silence. This led early sailors to believe Bermuda was an isle of devils, echoing with the screaming spirits of shipwrecked sailors.

Upon settlement, however, thousands of these passive black and white birds were clubbed to death on a regular basis to provide food – and delicious it was – to the colonists. By 1630, they were no more.

The 1951 discovery and subsequent nurturing has brought the numbers up to several hundred nesting primarily on the fiercely protected island of Nonsuch. It's not likely that you will ever see one, but you will hear a lot about them. Now you know the story.

The longtail is the other famous Bermuda bird. It too is black and white, but with a very long slim tail. These birds live all their lives (10 to 20 years) on the open ocean, but nest in crevasses in Bermuda's coastal cliffs. Regarded as the traditional harbinger of Spring, you may see them gliding around the beach areas in this season. If you see one flying above the other, touching their long tails together, you are witnessing their fascinating aerial courtship. Bermudian bachelors also identify with "longtailing". This is the expression used when dating tourist girls! The longtail bird is a marketing dream – depicted on souvenirs as varied as T-shirts, earrings and plates. Tourists love them – the birds, the souvenirs!

Now here's another weird story. Bermuda had some bad bugs that were killing the cedar trees so they brought in some good bugs (ladybugs) to eat the bad bugs. But, the lizards started eating the ladybugs so in 1957, a bird from Trinidad was brought in to eat the lizards. This bird was the kiskadee and, of course, everything thrives in Bermuda so they too got out of hand. Before Hurricane Emily, our yard provided a home to a dozen kiskadees. Where they went, I don't know, but I was happy to have them gone. About the size of a robin, and a gorgeous yellow color, these birds made a Sunday morning sleep-in virtually impossible. Their screeching, sounding exactly like their name, was enough to drive a person bananas. They also had an habit of dive-bombing the cat. Seriously. I saw this dozens of times while hanging clothes on the line. Of all the dead birds my cats presented to me, never once was one a kiskadee.

Another nuisance is the sparrow. When I had my chickens, I also had many of these (no doubt resulting from the constant food supply). These particular birds had a dreadful problem with mites, which they passed on to both my chickens and me. These horrid little bugs immediately led me to another round of research and chore number 821, regular "dusting" of my chickens with Malathion® powder.

Two of the prettiest birds are the cardinal and bluebird. The bright red male cardinal is unmistakable; the female is a rather basic brown. The bluebird receives much attention. Nesting boxes, purposely placed and regularly monitored by enthusiastic residents, have given them a new chance to flourish.

Unknown to many, the barn owl has a sizable population here. This large (14 - 20") bird of prey serves a very useful purpose; his diet consists mainly of rats. I was sure we had several owls in our yard until I found that the source of the cooing was a pair of mourning doves.

There are many fine sites to visit if you are interested in birds. Try Warwick Pond, Spittal Pond, the parks or the railway trail.

BEEPING

Midnight, July 1984: "Mother, would you PLEASE shut those birds up!"

When I first arrived, number 2,478 on my list of things to figure out was the source of this infernal night noise. I knew it wasn't birds – birds don't sing all night. I didn't relate this to Cassy though. Birds seemed a comforting explanation. Who knew what evils lurked out there in the night?

The ratio of sound volume to body weight is another one of those wonders of nature. This is found in the wail of a newborn baby or the screeching of a distressed chick. It is also found in Bermuda's tree frogs. These little guys, about the size of a fingernail, produce the unmistakable sounds of summer nights. Thousands, perhaps millions, begin "beeping", once the sun sets and they carry on until sunrise. This racket extends throughout the warm months, especially after a rain. At first, it may drive you crazy, but just as the mind tunes out train noises if one lives close to train tracks, it tunes out these sounds of summer. After a few weeks, you will only hear them if the topic is mentioned in conversation – which will happen EVERYTIME you have guests! Unless you go on a night search with a flashlight, it's not likely you will ever even see one. But, hear them you will – guaranteed. I like them, they're ... cute.

CHAMELEONS

A scream, followed by the verbalisation of my name, came from the cottage. Oh brother, now what? Investigation proved the source of this fuss was a chameleon, on the pillow, on the bed. Innkeeper job number 62: remove chameleons from pillows.

Actually, there are no chameleons here. What we have are four kinds of lizard – one native and three introduced. The "expats" were brought in to eat the roaches (here we go again!). One of these, from Antigua, was released in Warwick Parish and became known as the Warwick Lizard. It's famous because it can grow to 18", has a ridged crest on its head and looks a bit like a dragon. Now, I live in Warwick and have spent many hours prowling the "jungles", but I've never come face to face with one this size. It's doubtful you will either. What you will see are the other two. The Jamaican lizard is the camouflage expert, changing from purple to green to black. The Barbados lizard is usually green and found mainly in Somerset. These two are 6 to 8" long and not scary at all. The native lizard, found only here, is called the Bermuda Skink. It differs from the others in that its skin is smooth and claws take the place of suckers on its feet. They are 6 to 10" long and are now quite scarce. Without the suckers to help them out of discarded jars and cans and bottles, litter proves to be their grave.

I like these prehistoric critters too. They eat bugs! I wouldn't mind having a few live in the house to do just that, but they never survive inside. Occasionally I find one on the windowsill, dead and dried to a crisp. I suppose they need the moisture of the rain and dew. My cat thinks of them as gifts. While they can lose a tail by wiggling out of it, they don't often survive two fangs through the body. This is generally how they are presented to me, courtesy of Tuxedo, the cat. Luckily, he doesn't eat them. Presumably he thinks I do!

Liver flukes can result when a cat dines on lizards or tree frogs. This is quite a story. Snails ingest the eggs of the fluke parasite. Inside the snail these eggs become immature flukes which emerge through the skin. A lizard or frog ingests these and then, in turn, is eaten by a cat. This completes the cycle – once inside the cat, flukes mature, reproduce and the eggs are excreted with the feces. Then, it begins again. One would think this complex life cycle, dependent on three living hosts, wouldn't have a chance of becoming established. Nature is a wondrous thing. Tests done by the Department of Agriculture on trapped wild cats show a high level of infestation. If you have a "lizard-eater", inform your vet and have the cat checked regularly for these flukes. They are seldom deadly but, obviously, parasites living in your pet is a situation to avoid.

GOPHERS

Only once have I discovered one in the house. An open door one hot summer night was an invitation. I shooed him out with a broom and that was the end of it.

Often I am questioned about the inhabitants of the holes in the ground near the beach. Gophers? No – crabs. The Red Land Crab to be exact.

On their way to the sea, many of these fist-sized creatures fall prey to a gauntlet of automobiles. At least once a year, around midnight, on days following a full moon, the females must make this dangerous trek to the shore. Here, in the shallow water, they release about 100,000 larvae. While driving down South Road on these hot summer evenings, keep a lookout and watch where you're going. Don't destroy the new generation under your wheels.

If, unlike myself, you have no great compassion for creatures big and small – allow them to live for the races. Yes, the races. I thought that would get your attention.

Crab races are often an entertaining addition to summer beach parties. A bucket of crabs, each marked with a number on his back, is dumped, upside down in the middle of a previously marked circle. The crabs, totally confused, hightail it out of there, towards the edge of this circle. The first one to reach it, wins. Bets are taken prior to the race; some win, some lose and the profits generally go to a charity of some sort.

I don't recall seeing crabs in winter. They must hibernate, or whatever crabs do. Perhaps their food supply – grasses, seeds, palmetto berries, tree frogs, toads, dead birds – becomes scarce. In any case, since my arrival I've noticed that the crabs themselves are becoming scarce. I entreat you to be careful with them, their days are numbered.

CHAPTER EIGHT

Hunting Tiny Game

WAR

In my heart of hearts I did not want war. Pain, death, destruction – it was against everything I believed in. I had to do my utmost to avoid this. But, I had to do something. I did. I arranged a summit.

It went well. I was elated with my progress! We were able to agree on two points. First, we both had an equal right to the universe. Second, we must find a way to exist happily together. I had the answer. I would agree not to live in their house, if they would agree not to live in mine. The balance of the world would be open territory for both of us.

The peace treaty was signed.

I kept my side of the bargain but the opposing troops did not. Persevere, Tracey, persevere. I called a second summit.

After no end of discussion, the problem became clear. I had four in my army; the opposition had 14 billion. Control of each individual in this multitude was impossible. It only stood to reason that, sooner or later, rascals, renegades and radicals would cross the line in the sand. The Supreme Commander could not be held personally responsible for each and every one of them. And one of them – one ant, one roach, one flea – was one too many. I was left no alternative. I declared war.

As is always the case, the saints pay for the sinners.

ARTISTRY

It looked like a pencil line, many yards long, going up, down, across, something like a map or graph. What were these hieroglyphics? What did they mean? Who had been in our house, creating this geometric wonder on the kitchen wall?

Another mystery. But, wait, a clue. The line ended at the cat food dish. Oh my Lord, the line was moving – it was alive! Realization dawned. This line was the busy bodies of several thousand ants. Good grief!

Ants were here prior to 1622. Exactly how that happened would be a fascinating story but unfortunately, I don't know it.

Food, savoury or sweet, left out in the summer months will produce this phenomenon. Guaranteed. First, you will see one ant running around furiously searching for something edible. He is the scout. Once he makes the discovery, he hightails it back to the nest, holds a pow-wow and leads – by way of his scent – a raiding party back by exactly the same trail. Single file, thousands strong, they march across the walls, rugs, curtains – whatever is in their path. *Voilà!* The artistry of nature.

Most of us would just as soon forego this moving display. Do that by keeping food tightly covered or in the fridge in summer. And (ho hum) keep things clean. Remove used pet dishes immediately, rinse these dishes and your own. Clean up any crumbs, grains of sugar or fingerprints of peanut butter and jam as soon as you see them. Vacuum under couch cushions for bits of potato chips or cookie crumbs. In their search for the edible, the ants will also check you out. You will feel the bite, but it won't cause you any harm. These are very small (but determined) ants.

When I find one of these ant trails in my home, I remove the food source which confuses the heck out of them. Then, they just go back where they came from. Bug spray just makes another mess – thousands of now sticky and poisonous dead ants to clean up. Spraying will, however, destroy that route for awhile. But, they will find another. Through the wall plug is a popular choice. As always, I did my tests and observations on this problem too.

The Bermuda cedar tree, famed for its bug repellant properties, seemed a good place to start – environmentally sensible as it was. I asked my son to bring home all the cedar chips from his woodworking class. I stuffed these into old nylon stockings and tied the ends. I put them in drawers and closets. It smelled wonderful and I never did find a bug of any sort in these spaces. My problem was solved. Not quite. Over time, the oil remaining in this wood spotted my linens. The chips emitted sawdust that coated everything. This was a real pain. So much for that plan. Next? Herbs, also known for their repellent qualities. Also messy.

About this time I entered a phase of my life characterized by a totally fed-up attitude regarding research, experiments, trials, observations and conclusions. I simply had to have a vacation from all this scientific stuff. This was also the time I heard about the famous boric acid treatment. But, I had temporarily thrown in the towel, I couldn't deal with it. Instead, I handed the problem over to the experts – a pest control company. This solution was expensive; it was smelly; it was effective. If you decide to go this route, make the appointment once the heat and humidity set in, in May or June. A man comes in, sprays the bottom half of the inside walls, around all windows and doors and anywhere else that might serve as a good hideout. He also sprays the outside of the house and an area of ground up to the foundation. This is a good day to go out. Stay away a few hours to let the solution dry and then open all the windows to air the place out. At this point, forget about Spring cleaning. The more of the chemical left in the corners and on the baseboards and windows the better – there is no point in cleaning it off. Once an insect walks over any of these areas, his hours are numbered. There's a great satisfaction in knowing that even if you see one on the run, it's game over. No mating, no eggs, no flying around – finished. If you find yourself involved in a constant battle with bugs, this may be the way to go, a cost of living in paradise.

For any number of reasons, you may not want to choose this route. After a few years, the thought of spraying poison all around my house seemed to be conflicting just a tad with my studies of Buddhism. What I chose instead was to do my level best to encourage biological control by Bermuda's other critters, especially the toads. To this end, daughter Cassy even presented me with a toad house one Mother's Day.

Again, this may not be your choice. If you would like to try the boric acid treatment, I'll tell you how. Buy boric acid at the drugstore. Determine which species of ant you have (don't panic, there are only two). If they have a huge head (easily discernable), they prefer protein. If they don't have this huge head, they're Argentinian and prefer sweet foods. The purpose of this exercise is to determine the bait. For the big-headed type use cat/dog food, butter or peanut butter; for Argentinians – honey or jam. Mix the bait and boric acid 20 to 1 and place about 1/4 tsp. at intervals around the perimeter of your house. As the bait disappears, replace it. Do this for several days. As the poisoned food is transported back to the nest and fed to the queen, reproduction ceases. You should notice a substantial drop in their number after this. I never did try it, but I've heard a dozen reports that it works well.

If you have children or pets and want to take the safest route, other reports suggest pouring boiling water on outside nests and blocking inside points of entry with talcum powder or red chili pepper.

Terror

What worried me most was the terror they invoked. I was sure, one way or another, they would be the end of me. Perhaps, while driving one day, I would pull down the sun visor and one would fall in my lap. That would do it; I'd be over a cliff somewhere. Death by cockroach.

I had to get a grip on this. I knew it was irrational. They were not dangerous. They could not hurt me. What exactly was my problem? Given a choice, why was it that I would rather run into a bear?

I began a quest to conquer this fear of cockroaches. I had a long nature talk with myself. As living things, didn't they have as much right to this planet as I did? They had been around for 350 MILLION years. Despite man's best efforts to eradicate the entire species, they were still here. Accept what you cannot change. And so on.

This approach did not work. So, with a sigh, I moved on. Plan B.

I had already established it was not so much the knowledge of their presence but, rather, the actual sighting of them that was so disgusting. A clue. I went to work on that.

I asked Scott to put a dead roach in a jar. My plan was to look at that little devil enough times to desensitize my mind and eyes to this sight (something like watching violence on TV). Sounded good to me. Well, let me just say, I would have had this roach ornament decorating my home for years. I gave up these mind games and decided to concentrate on prevention.

I covered every container. I did the dishes immediately, I vacuumed up every crumb. I sprayed bug killer around every window and door and I cleaned cupboards constantly. If I saw one, alive or dead, in the day, I ran outside and got one of my chickens. That roach was history. Chickens love roaches. By accident I discovered that my long-necked crystal decanter was a perfect trap – roaches could get in but they couldn't get out. Following this clue, I put out oily and sticky type foods. This caught them and held them fast, but every ant in the parish came in for the honey or jam or peanut butter.

These measures were not producing the results I sought. Back to research. I asked every acquaintance what they knew about this. They filled me with information and advice: the flying ones are the females, the small ones are the worst, they make noises, don't turn on the lights at night – then you won't see them, bang on the cupboard before you open it – they will run and hide. I was getting nowhere fast and, as I went along, I found much of what they told me was simply not true. I went to the library. I borrowed two volumes. This wasn't fast either, but it was fruitful. It took me three months to wade through hundreds of pages of scientific mumbo jumbo, but I gathered much useful information.

I learned how to recognize the different types, the eggs, the excrement. In my opinion, the American Roach is the worst. It's black and it's huge. The size has something to do with the fear – tiny roaches don't give me chills. I'm not crazy about the German one either, but it's smaller and brown. I'm always on the lookout for the eggs – 3/4", brown, segmented, rod-shaped packages of trouble. I find them stuck in the corners of picture frames, furniture, books, cupboards. Dispose of them immediately. I'm also on the lookout for ... poop. It's a summer morning ritual now – throwing a cursory glance over the kitchen counters in search of very small, rod-shaped, black pieces of evidence. If it's there, a roach is slumbering away his day in a crack or crevice somewhere nearby. Check the cracks and crevices keeping a sharp eye out for two long, brown antennae (which usually don't fit into the hiding spots). Failing this, turn off the light in the kitchen at night and wait awhile. Return to the kitchen, flick on the light and quickly scour the room. In both these cases, have a can of bug spray handy. The tiniest squirt will do it, just give that bug one quick shot and put the can over it. Then, go do something else for a few hours. When hubby comes home, have HIM arrange the burial.

I also learned of a strange food source: glue – wallpaper glue, furniture glue, the wheat paste used to bind old books. This explained why my books, printed prior to 1940, were falling apart. I also learned that a favourite food of roaches is cinnamon buns (not that this was much help).

I learned that they needed warmth (hot water heaters, ovens, closet heaters, summer temperatures), water (the kitchen and bathroom) and a high humidity environment (Bermuda!). Their transport around this hospitable environment was provided by boxes, soda packs, bags. (One always comes in with the Christmas decorations, stored in the garage. The Christmas Roach.)

I learned of their predators: lizards, toads, the ensign wasp. I considered PET lizards and toads. I never identified an ensign wasp, but

I hope I have lots in my house. *They* lay *their* eggs in cockroach egg cases. When the wasps hatch, they eat the unhatched roaches encapsulated in the same nest. Disgusting, but effective.

While all this was going on, I became increasingly aware of my senses. The capacity for the eye to see movement is incredible. If it moved, I saw it, but nevertheless, roaches constantly caught me by surprise. This was the unnerving element of their presence. Let me cover this by stating that until you have had a peek do not slip your hands into a pair of oven mitts or ... rubber gloves.

As I walked down the hall one day, movement in the bedroom caught my eye. I was surprised to see, Paul ... prancing. Now, let me state here that Paul is not a prancer, or a dancer or given to flights of fancy of ANY kind. What was going on here? Out of his pant leg crawled an American roach (the big one). Had that been me ... well, I shudder to think. Paul also found one in the toilet paper roll – another shuddering thought. Being Bermudian, he is not possessed by my panic – given the choice, his opponent would NOT be the bear.

Now that we have replaced most of our windows, installed air conditioning and encouraged toad residency, our roach problems have decreased dramatically. If you find you need heavy-duty control, you can always call the pest control company. A thorough job will last three months. (They only guarantee a month but trust me, it's three.) This will pretty well get you through the summer. Winter is not a problem – they disappear. No, I don't know where to – hibernating, I guess. I don't much care where they go. Heck, I'd pack their bags.

FLEAS

1994

I marched into the office, looked directly into his eyes and emphatically stated, "I will NOT have FLEAS in my house!" He smiled. Those were the days when I still believed I could control my world. I was the recipient of many of these smiles my first few years in Bermuda. Translation: "Good luck lady." This time *he* was the vet.

If you have pets, you will have fleas. Sorry. You can try commercial flea collars and ones made of rope – dipped in the oil of the herbs pennyroyal, eucalyptus or lavender. You can try flea shampoo, spray or foam. You can "bomb" the house, catch them in trays of soapy water left on the floors of every room, vacuum every day or put moth balls in the vacuum bag. You can practise your hand to eye co-ordination by spending all evening picking them off one by one with a vaseline-covered cotton swab or a pair of tweezers. You can make your pet's bed of cedar chips. You can give your pet flea pills or brewer's yeast three times a week but ... you will still have fleas.

Theoretically, it is possible to rid your home and property of every single flea – for a moment. That moment will pass when a wild cat takes a stroll through your yard. That moment will pass when the eggs (hidden in carpets, sofas, blankets, cracks and crevices) move on to the next stage in their life cycle.

A flea is a true wonder of nature, perfectly created, with survival skills beyond measure. He is smaller than an ant, about the size of a pinhead. His bristly body, flattened sideways, and his clawed feet allow easy movement through thick fur and the ability to remain attached to the fastest moving host. He can pull 400 times his own weight and jump 120 times his length. If his food supply dries up, he goes into a state of suspended animation. He can survive this way for over a year. His mouth is a tool kit. It contains a "saw" to pierce the skin, a hollow tube to access the blood and a "pump" to extract it. In nine months, under ideal conditions, a pair of fleas can produce *trillions* more. Good grief, no wonder they've been around for eons!

The success of this march through the ages is due, in no small part, to a four-stage life cycle: egg, larva, cocoon and adult. Depending on environmental conditions, this cycle can complete itself in three weeks or up to two years. A female, who will lay 300 - 500 eggs in her lifetime, releases three to eighteen white waxy eggs on or off the host. She's not fussy. These eggs look exactly like grains of salt and will be everywhere your pet is or has been. Two to four weeks later, the larvae emerge.

Flea larvae look like ... well ... larvae – small, *very small*, cream-coloured, worm-like, moving bits of life. For 9 to 200 days, they wiggle around eating dirt, dead skin cells, flea droppings, disgusting-type stuff. In this same period they also moult twice. On the third moult, they enter the cocoon stage where they remain from seven days to a year. Then, *voilà!* A footstep, a pawstep, a vibration, and in an instant the cocoon bursts open to reveal one very hungry flea.

Your first clue that all this is taking place, right under your nose, will be one of the following: "salt" (eggs) and "pepper" (poop) in your pet's bedding or wherever he sleeps; hair loss or sores on your pet's skin (brought on by incessant scratching); a collection of tiny red spots (blood) anywhere when the humidity is high; small pink, itchy dots below your knee level.

Flea droppings look like tiny, black, curled hairs. When these are supplied with moisture (high humidity), they release a telltale sign that one who eats red will excrete red. Sweep up these droppings as soon as you see them. When left to become liquid, they are as difficult to remove as blood.

A severe flea infestation may cause anemia, especially in long-haired white pets. For some reason fleas are attracted to this colour. Our white, long-haired cat had no end of problems, but the grey, short-haired one wasn't much bothered. Some pets are allergic to the chemicals flea saliva releases. This can result in hair loss and sores. To handle these complications, see your vet.

Below-the-knee spots on YOU are also the result of a slight reaction to this saliva. You've been bitten. It's not likely that you will feel the bite, but it will itch later. The best comparison I can make is to mosquitoes. They both bite and itch and are a darned nuisance but, in Bermuda at least, they don't cause major problems. In our house, I'm the one they like. Cassy tells me this is because – somewhat like fine wine – fleas prefer "aged" blood. Comforting, she is. There may be something to this though. Mom spent her vacation here, helping me make preserves. She went home loaded down with loquat cake, jam, chutney and quite a case of "measles" on both her calves!

As I'm sure you've gathered by now, my study of fleas was pretty intense. Know your enemy. Flea reproduction is at its strongest in a 65 - 80 degree temperature and a 70% humidity level. Now, what place does this describe? For the first eight years, my experimenting boiled down to the following multi-pronged attack: regular bathing with flea shampoo for the long-haired cat, flea foam for the short-haired one; twice weekly vacuuming of all floors and furniture; a visit from the pest control company in Spring; the addition of moth balls to the vacuum cleaner bag; and last, but most important, weekly combing with a flea comb.

The latter two suggestions came from the vet who, by this time, probably thought I was writing a thesis on fleas! All the vacuuming results in the accumulation of hundreds of flea eggs in the vacuum cleaner bag. This dark, dirty, food-filled environment serves as a perfect incubator for the hatching of larvae. A couple of mothballs in the bag every couple of weeks solves this. For a short time after you vacuum, your house will smell of mothballs; when this no longer happens, add a few more. The flea comb is a wonderful invention! It looks like a silver comb, but has teeth very, very close together. This little miracle removes fleas, droppings and eggs. After each stroke, dip the comb in soapy water or alcohol and wipe it with a paper towel. One session with it sold me. Get one and you'll feel the same. Be sure you get the right one, it should have a handle and be made of metal.

2002

Now, for the best invention since sliced bread! The foregoing information was important for you to read to establish a true appreciation for a product called Advantage™. Incredible stuff! Get it from the vet. Put a thin line of it on the back of your pet's neck once a month. No fleas, no more. Honestly. All the above nonsense: the work, the aggravation, the explanations to guests ended 24 hours after my discovery of this wonder product. There is no downside. If you have a dog, a cat, get it, use it.

CHAPTER NINE

It's a Jungle Out There!

TREES

"Well now you've done it; you've killed it. All I asked you to do was give it a little water. Of course, you know this means our marriage is doomed!"

Bermuda wedding tradition dictates that a young Bermuda cedar tree be placed on the top tier of the wedding cake and then should be planted by the bride and groom during the reception. If it grows, so will their love. The foregoing was my spiel to Paul sometime in the early 80's. I had just returned from a summer trip to find Paul had not watered our cedar tree and it had bitten the dust. So, not only were we late in planting ours (which had never been on any cake), but now it was dead. This did not bode well.

In the beginning, prior to 1609, Bermuda was a virtual forest of evergreen, coniferous, cedar trees. Colonisation resulted in an unbridled use of this rich, red-coloured wood for furniture, houses and boats. As early as the 1700's, conservation was indicated and implemented. This worked well until the 1940's. Around that time, two parasitic scale insects were inadvertently imported with some California trees. In less than 10 years, the cedar forests were decimated.

Government, in an effort to reforest the Island, chose the Australian casuarina as a replacement. These trees are fast growing, tolerant of shallow limestone soil and cold, salty winter winds. However, they drop their needles and pinecone-like seeds on roads, driveways and roofs which eventually find their way into water tanks. In severe storms, they uproot easily and create quite a mess, being (at maturity) sixty or seventy feet tall. For these reasons, they are no longer the tree of choice. Old Hurricane Emily brought many casuarinas down – housecleaning by nature.

Another nuisance tree is the Mexican pepper – it grows and spreads rapidly, in all directions. While we have recently begun efforts to rid our property of these trees, they do offer a perfect sanctuary for birds. These are the trees my chickens always chose to sleep in. These are the only trees my chicks were able to climb until their wings had strengthened enough to get them to the top in one burst. In December, clusters of red berries, perfect for flower arrangements, appear.

The stately Norfolk pine seems out of place to me. It looks more like a Christmas tree. We have three of these. I worry about the day they come down; they're huge!

Our perfectly shaped Frangipani fell over in the famous "Emily" escapade. We put it back up, anchored it down and along came Hurricane Dean. Over it went again. I cut it in pieces and planted it, as it was (no roots, just bits of branches) all over the yard. Some took hold and survived, much to my amazement.

About nine years ago, I picked up a leaf I found while walking along South Road. I was so impressed by its size that I brought it home and tacked it over the verandah door. It's still there. This leaf came from the bay grape tree. It grows wild along South Road, its leathery leaves resistant to the hot and cold salty winds from the ocean. Clusters of green, then purple, grapes appear in summer. Once purple, they can be eaten as is or made into jelly.

Bermuda's unique and fragrant landscape is created by so many endemic and specially chosen trees that I can't begin to give details on them all. Do a study yourself or get in on one of the Botanical Garden Tours - it's fascinating stuff!

PLANTS

Landscaped? Now there's a good question. I suppose it was, some forty or so years ago. Nature has since taken over though and, despite our efforts, the vegetation surrounding our home is basically wild. I have always (lovingly) called it "the jungle."

Our third of an acre contains ... oh ... about a hundred varieties of plants. Horticulturally illiterate as I was, establishing the name (never mind the properties) of each species was a daunting task. Ho hum, more research.

Upon arrival, I thought the bluebell was gorgeous. I was horrified when my brother-in-law said it had to go. No! I was keeping it! Time proved him right. This plant grows at the speed of light, strangling all greenery in its path, including trees. Our yard was a profusion of blue-bells (and strangled plants). The bluebell vines were the diameter of a thumb; Cassy and Scott could swing through the trees, playing Tarzan, with them. Their removal took two years.

Many of my plants: dieffenbachia, oleander, lantana, poinsettia, are poisonous or have attributes that cause physical distress. The chick-ens ate all my Purple Heart plants which is just as well. The sap causes stinging, itching and a rash. This just goes to show – don't mimic chickens! For more information on poisonous varieties, especially if you have small children, buy *The Be Careful Book of Plants in Bermuda.* Many of my plants are edible: nasturtium, Locust-and-Wild-Honey, Natal plum, loquat, fennel, paw-paw. My peach tree is obviously in dire need of help; each year it produces a total crop of five peaches. I spent an entire winter trying to make a palatable juice from the fruit of my bitter orange tree. No luck. Marmalade seems to be the only suitable use for this citrus.

Many of my plants make great flower arrangements: narcissus, pittosporum, Norfolk pine, Mexican pepper, shrimp plant, rubber tree. Most hibiscus, however, only last a few hours once cut. Any woody-stemmed plant must have the stem crushed (to increase water absortion) or it won't last either. Be cautious with plants exuding a milky sap, most will produce a stinging or otherwise unpleasant skin sensation.

I should mention here Bermuda's flower, the Bermudiana. This endemic perennial resembles a miniature iris, growing 12 - 18 inches high with five or six purple petals. It appears, growing wild, in April. A pictorial representation is found on china plates; its fragrance is captured in a perfume named (appropriately enough) Bermudiana.

Speaking of perfume ... Bermuda has a Perfumery producing scents from those flowers grown on the property: frangipani, passion flower, lily and more. Take a tour, wander the grounds, then see how the perfumes are produced. Buy a sampler set to find your favorite fragrance. Buy several – these testers also make great gifts.

CHAPTER TEN

The Body Politic

Torture & Weight

"Yes, madam, you can be tortured here – for a small fee!"

You can be kneaded and needled, plucked and powdered, wrapped and waxed, painted and primed, teased and sprayed. Whatever your particular brand of punishment, it's available. The beauty shops in town, the hotels and the health clubs supply these services. Check the prices; they do vary, but if you are accustomed to paying for these services, you will not find the costs prohibitive.

While I'm on the subject of pain for gain: You must keep yourself moving, preferably with an exercise program. The net result of all this slowing down, staying home, heat and humidity is prominently displayed on the body. I had an extra four pounds to show for each year I lived here. It sneaks up in the summer when it's too darned hot to run around in circles. In winter, the world shuts down at 5 p.m. All you want to do on those cold evenings is to cuddle under an afghan. This does not burn many calories. Neither does gourmet dining, a favourite form of entertainment here. Tea time with its wonderful selection of pastries is alive and well as are social events with selections of tasty but fattening nibbles. Yes, you must partake of some of these treats but do balance this with something physical. Just do it, or five years will get you twenty pounds. It did me. But, I'm pleased to report I lost it after a year of consistent exercise. It works. Honest. Thirty minutes three times a week on a bicycle will do it for you. That's not hard.

Actually, it's quite easy to be physically active in this country, especially in winter. Yoga, Pilates, and Tai Chi classes are offered. Several gyms in Hamilton and most major hotels offer memberships for residents to workout. Some of these include pool privileges. Of course, Bermuda's pool is the Atlantic Ocean – enjoy it: swimming, sailing, fishing, scuba diving. Join one of many clubs or start your own. How about golf? Or tennis? Take some lessons. Join a bowling club. Walk the railway trails with a friend – that's what I do – join us! For two years now, I have been walking the Paget railway trail with a small group of guys and gals. I certainly plan to continue so I will give you the details in the hope that if you want to come, we'll still be at it. You can always call me, I'm in the phone book. Monday to Friday we meet at 9 a.m. at the rear of the Modern Mart parking lot. We walk three miles in an hour – a beautiful, gentle walk.

SKIN

An old realtor pal of mine had devised an interesting business promotion angle. She sauntered around restaurants full of dining businessmen. She dropped her business card in front of each one and instructed them to put it in their glass of water. These cards, looking for all the world like pieces of regular business card paper, were, in fact, highly compressed pieces of sponge. The dumping in water swelled them to a sponge big enough to fill your hand lengthwise. This created quite a fuss resulting in each and every one of those men remembering her name and then some!

I had several of these business cards when I arrived here. A week later, without the aid of a glass of water, I had three sponges. Responding to the moisture in the air, they had swelled to their saturated size. This is exactly what happens to your skin. Allow this to happen by leaving the heavy-duty, oil-based creams in their jars – you will have no need for them. Instead, use a water-based light moisturizer for a base. Trade in your liquid foundation for powder. Powder soaks up excess oil, perspiration and the wet, sticky, shiny problems this climate fosters. Only one day after your arrival, you will notice an improvement in your skin. Dry, flaky, "crocodile" skin will disappear without the help of lotions – save them for your trips away. I spent my first week here removing face and hand cream from everything I touched; it just didn't sink in; it was all over my hair, clothes and everything else. Unless you are spending many hours in the sun or detergent solutions, "larding yourself up" is just a waste of time and "lard".

One square inch of skin contains 19 million cells. Guess what happens when each one of them gathers "just a touch" of extra moisture? Yep, you get bigger. You will notice this in your shoes and clothing, especially in summer when skin also expands for cooling purposes. Remember this if you shop "off island". I have four pair of shoes, bought away, that I can only wear when away. And one very fitted dress that I can only wear in Bermuda because I'm bigger here. No kidding.

Remember sunscreen. Lord, I can't go through this lecture one more time. You know it, right?

HAIR

I had always had long, thick, dry, wavy hair. Several hairdressers, over the years, had assured me that this was the ONLY kind of hair to have. Until I arrived here, I agreed. I could go for days without washing it; once curled, it remained exactly that way; there was always enough of it to create any style that took my fancy. I never, never, ever used mousse, gel, hairspray or sticky, mucky preparations of any kind and had no intention of ever doing so. I also refused to have it cut.

Two years into my Bermuda life, I gave up. I could spend one hour creating a masterpiece – it lasted ten minutes. Determination being one of my long suits, I repeated this procedure two hundred times. Swollen by all the absorbed moisture, I had twice as much hair as I came here with which was plenty in the first place; in summer it was perspiration-glued to my neck, shoulders, forehead, or back (any bare skin); the humidity gave me a style of permanent, wavy frizz. It was impossible!

I had it cut short. I used mousse. I used hairspray. I had it thinned. I broke every promise I had made to myself. After several years of friends and family gently explaining that this *wasn't me*, I let it grow again. I devised a system. In winter, it's down, to keep my neck warm; in summer, it's up out of the way. Mousse tames the frizzies and holds the style, while hairspray keeps the "up style" up.

I know you want me to tell you *how* to keep your hair in order under a helmet. I would *really* like to do that. I am reminded of one of our guests who came home from his first day at work in a most distressed state. Not only had his brand new tie gotten soaked in the rain, but his hair was *squished* by his helmet. Truly, I have never seen a full-grown man carry on so. Exhausted after two hours of trying to calm him down, I then handed him over to Paul who did another two hours' worth. I suppose we can say it was an evening well spent as, years later, he's still in Bermuda. Sometimes you just need someone to talk to.

ANYWAY, getting back to my solutions for "helmet hair", I don't have any. Sorry. Accept the things you cannot change.

DRESS

Where I come from, a pair of jeans will take you just about anywhere. Not so here. When I first arrived, I was fascinated by the children. How they managed to look so well-manicured, even when dressed head-to-toe in whites, totally bewildered me. Whether on the street by our house, in town or at any event, these little tykes looked as though they had just stepped out of a magazine! Beautifully braided hair held ribbons and bows that matched their outfits which matched their spotless shoes. How was this done?

The answer was quite simple: Bermudians share a strong pride in cleanliness. This shows in the clean streets, parks and constant war against litter. It is also seen in their dress. Raised from early childhood to this standard, it remains with them for life. Even school uniforms are mandatory resulting in adults who not only know *how* to tie a tie but also how to look smart, sporty, professional and always well-turned-out.

The business attire for men takes some getting used to. Bermuda shorts with a suit jacket and tie is still a strange sight for me to behold. Pink, lime green and canary yellow shorts, ties and socks (on a man) is a bit jarring at first. If your hubby is a bit of an adventurous spirit, and decides to *dress Bermudian,* keep in mind this critical fashion error: wearing anything but knee-length socks with Bermuda shorts. It is simply not done. Of course, a regular suit (with long pants) is perfectly acceptable. Upscale restaurants may insist on jacket and tie after 6 p.m.; check with them when making reservations. Naked chests, anywhere but the beach, are illegal. Yes, illegal. The same goes for very short shorts and swimsuits. Advise your mate to cover up. Ladies, save your thong bikini for the Mediterranean – not permitted. Smart casual does NOT include jeans, track suits, running shoes or flip-flops.

While dress-down days have come to Bermuda and slacks are now acceptable, business clothes for women remain at a professional level. Individuality is not encouraged. Leave your outlandish costumes at home. As a businesswoman, most of your day will be spent in a controlled environment (with air conditioning or heat). Fabrics, textures and styles need not change with the seasons. (Actually, you will probably need a sweater in the office in the summer. For reasons I can't fathom, most offices are kept far too cool in the hot months.) If you are not career-oriented, stick with the following: in summer wear as little as morally decent; in winter wear as much as you can comfortably work in. For more elaboration on this see the sections on summer and winter.

CHAPTER ELEVEN

Mind Over Matter

ADJUSTMENT

If, like many, you have just married or left a career behind, I empathize. I did both. MAJOR adjustment. At "home", I had seen and spoken with fifty people before noon, every day. Here, by 8 a.m., I was alone and remained that way until 6 p.m. Paul had an exciting new job; Cassy and Scott had exciting new schools complemented by half a dozen extracurricular activities. Here I was, with the cat, the mildew, a phone that never rang and no one to call. It was hot and lonely. It was the pits! It was adjustment time.

These feelings and emotions are completely normal in this situation. I had recognized that long before I left Canada and even went so far as to tell my friends not to ask how I liked Bermuda until one year had elapsed. I don't adapt well; I don't adjust well; I'm not that crazy about change, or, as the diplomats put it, *progress*. I knew this would be a struggle. It's important to realize that a move to a new country ranks pretty high on the stress scale and that, whoever you are, whatever your strengths, there will be some tough times. Accept this and you're halfway there. We've all been through it. We've all felt the same. Remember, stress creates a diamond from a lump of coal. There will be times you'll feel stressed to the max. BUT ... (this is the important point) ... how else can you become a diamond?

Okay, I had established that the first year would be a rough one. Now, the question was: what was I going to do about it?

Step one: identify the problem. This was quite a list: no friends, no family, no driver's license, too much housework, no time for me, too hot, too humid, boxes everywhere, no mental stimulation, etc., etc., etc. I had always prided myself on being independent but I was out of my element. I didn't know ANYTHING: where to go, how to get there, what was there once I arrived, the rules, the prices, the standards. Okay, I thought, we'll start with that. Finding out.

Step two: how? I read the newspaper, the tourist brochures, the pamphlets from the Bermuda College and the Community Courses guide. I joined the library; I ordered the information brochures the government puts out. I walked every street in town, wandered around the neighbourhood, took a few bus rides. I studied the map as Paul drove around. I began my driving lessons. This all took quite some time and kept me busy the first year. I didn't know which was worse, my list of problems or my list of solutions, but I got started. That's the important thing, to just get at it. None of this will come to you. Take the initiative and *do it.* I'm still at it but it's comfortable now. Year One is the one to survive. Give yourself at least this much time, it's only fair ... to you ... and to Bermuda.

AUSTRALIA

August 3, 1992: 4 a.m.

My memory just dug this one up. More proof that I belong to the realm of nocturnal beings. Actually, I had a coffee at midnight. Bad plan. I've been to bed every hour, on the hour since. Obviously, without results. Well, not quite. I have this story to share with you. Also, in case you're interested, it's 81 degrees in the kitchen at this ungodly hour.

I met Lorraine in Canada in the early 80's. She needed a house; I was a realtor. A mutual friend put us together. By the time the business transactions were completed, we were good friends. I learned a lot from this lady, much of it applies here.

Lorraine's husband had accepted an engineering contract for work in my province. He and Lorraine had made the major decision, with two children in tow, to move. From AUSTRALIA, no less! At the time, I thought THAT was pretty amazing. But, there was lots more to follow.

The major thrust of the work was centered around a little tourist town in the mountains. After a short time, they rented a place up there. Poor Lorraine, now she didn't even have the comfort of the few friends she had made in the city. Poor Lorraine nothing! This is what Lorraine did. She found a niche and filled it. She made Pavlova.

Pavlova is a specialty Australian dessert containing meringue, fruit and whipped cream. Delicious! And this is exactly what the restaurants – in this little tourist town – thought. She approached them and offered to make and sell them this "little bit of Australia". Big hit.

Before long she was up to her eyeballs in Pavlova and knee deep in egg yolks. Meringue requires egg whites only. What to do? She stopped and thought for a bit. (Stop and think.) Aha! She had it! Italians! Italian cooking requires the use of yolks and yolks only. Back to the streets. Back to the restaurants - the Italian ones. Sure enough, they were throwing out their egg whites and were quite happy to swap their whites for her yolks.

Now think about this for a moment. Here was this lost and lonely lady in unfamiliar surroundings, bored and unproductive and unsatisfied. A little concentrated thought, a few trips to town, motivation and a never-say-die attitude turned this picture around. She was working, using her own hands and skills, creating, busy, in touch with people, filling a void, treating the residents to a new taste sensation. She was recycling, saving perfectly good food from becoming part of the daily trash. And she was making money. All this with very few tools and very little outlay.

I am not recommending that you start selling Pavlova. For one thing, meringue and humidity are deadly enemies. Also, you would need a work permit (and a tiled kitchen and a high-heat dishwasher and ...). However, my purpose in relating this story is to show how a sweet shy schoolteacher from Australia took stock of a problem, found a solution and implemented it. It was a good lesson for me. I was SO impressed. Try to use some of her wisdom to help you through your rough spots. I know she'd be honoured if you did.

A few years into my Bermuda life, I received a call from Australia. It was Lorraine. She wanted me to meet her in Montana for a ski week. Not likely. She was not daunted by this response. After her ski week, she hopped on a plane, flew to Bermuda and visited me here. What a gal!

SWIZZLES

Every new resident and visitor asks me the same question, "What do you DO here?" I am always tempted to confirm their suspicions by replying, "Oh, I just spend my days sitting under palm trees drinking rum swizzles."

There is this belief, in the *real* world, that if you live in Bermuda, this (and golfing) is all we do here. I am now at the point where I avoid telling anyone from abroad where I live. If I do, I know I'm in for no end of *oohing* and *aahing*. Then comes the standard 500 questions one would ask "a lady of leisure from Paradise". I just can't go through it one more time.

Some years we don't get to the beach. I know, it's sacrilege. BUT, when you live here, you are NOT a tourist. You spend your days doing what everyone else, all over the world, spends their days doing – dealing with the day-to-day matters of life. This is one good reason to have visitors; it forces you to stop, change tracks and enjoy the simple pleasures this country offers. This is good advice for any local from any country, but most will not experience the volume of visitors a Bermuda resident receives, and other countries have rental cars. Visitors tend to go off on their own more often. These facts are unknown to those who question what I do with my time.

They also do not realize how family moves into a whole new realm – both those here with you and those back home. Those who have joined you need lots of love, time and attention to ease THEIR adjustment. Those you have left become even more special. Absence makes the heart grow fonder. You have embarked on an exciting new adventure and everyone wants to share it! You, of course, are homesick, lonely and missing their presence. Letters, e-mails, telephone calls, gifts and trips home help to ease this emptiness. All of this takes time.

In the many facets of life here, these are but two of the things I *do*. I have never been one to find boredom a problem. I know my life is *what I make it. I* am the master of my ship. *I* have choices. Boredom is a state of mind ... only *I* can change that. I never have enough time – ever. There's just *so much* I want to do ... to learn ... to be. There is just no way I am going to accomplish it all in this lifetime.

August 17, 1993

Paul was out mowing the lawn. Through the open window I heard him mumbling. Oh no! It was the "Holy Smokes" speech! I joined him outside. He pointed up. On the roof, waddling around, just as happy as you please, were two white GEESE! Job number 569: remove geese from roof.

November 15, 1993

Mooing. Oh no! Please, please, please – not a cow in the yard! More mooing. Why, oh why, did these things happen to me?

Gingerly, I peeked out the front door – nothing. The back door – nothing. Further investigation located the source of this communication, in a vacant field, across the road. At this point, I had the wary attention of not one, but two cows. I took this opportunity (job number 847) to forcefully explain that they were not, under any circumstances, to venture across the road; *Casscott* was off-limits to cows.

Practice makes perfect and I was elated to find my speech effective. There are no cows at *Casscott*.

ACTIVITIES

Your first few months in Bermuda will be busy ones: getting your nest in order, shopping, organizing papers and finding your way around. Most likely, before you have those jobs completed, family and friends will start arriving. You will be amazed at how many friends you have once you're living in paradise. This will be a busy time, made more so by the preparation before and the returning to normal after your guests leave.

Once life has settled into a pattern and you have a routine set up, think about what you would like to do. The list is endless: join a gym, do some volunteer work, be a beach bum, begin a walking program, take music, dance, art, tennis or golf lessons, enroll in some interest courses at the community centres or work towards a degree at the Bermuda College. Read books, learn about Bermuda, watch all the videos of shows you missed, see the sights. Once you make a few friends, choose a day and make it girls' day out – a day a week just to goof-off or, perhaps, to do something intellectual, whatever. Be selfish about this. Spend some time reflecting on all the times you have said, "Someday, I'd like to ..." or "If I had the time, I'd ...". It's someday NOW and you HAVE the time. As Cassy would say, "Get a life," or "Don't live in a lunchbox." Do things just for you. Treat yourself to a manicure, pedicure, facial, massage. Put some highlights in your hair; have a bubble bath. If the individual in you is happy, the wife and mother in you will be also. Do this for your family – be selfish.

You will find that housework takes up much more time than you're used to. About three times. Everything, and I mean everything, must be kept clean, moving and dry. Boring and monotonous housework is a universal problem. Try to make it fun, interesting, informative. Set your microwave timer and see just how long it takes to: iron a dozen shirts, wash the floors, clean the windows. Then, each week see if you improve. If you always vacuum from the front to the back of the house, reverse it. If you always vacuum the whole house, then dust the whole house, try completing one room at a time. Read your instruction manuals, see if you are, in fact, using and cleaning your appliances correctly. For instance, when was the last time you changed the fan belt on your vacuum? Put drain cleaner down the drains? Vacuumed the lint from under and behind your fridge? Cleaned out the dryer vent? Turned your mattress? Do some research, test three furniture polishes. Get into it, do it differently, test yourself.

Vegetation grows at the speed of light here. Many, many hours can be spent tending the yard. While you're out there, pick a few plants and try your hand at flower arranging. This is good for many hours! These beautiful handmade arrangements can fill the spots that your old brass ornaments previously occupied. If you own a home, there will never be an end to painting. The sun, salt, sand and sea take their toll.

Shopping is a major time consumer as well. You may need to go to three grocery stores for the week's menu and visit ten stores to find an item you need. You'll be driving all over the place. If you find the prices prohibitive, you may join the rest of the population in seeking out garage sales, auctions, second-hand stores. Chances are excellent that the fellow leaving has exactly what you're looking for and has it advertised in the newspaper or at one of the famous leaving-island-sales. Check them out.

Take time to read the newspaper and watch the news. Listen to the BBC for a change – interesting interviews and a decidedly differ-ent slant from U.S. news Be informed. Give yourself something intel-ligent to think about, like, just how serious your problems are com-pared with those in Bangladesh. I call this my culture hour. Mind work. Daily newspapers from overseas are available; do the daily crossword. More mind work. Give your mind an hour a day and give your body the same and give your spirit the same. We are tri-part beings. Allow balance and opportunity for each to grow

You will spend more time on yourself. Being *beautiful* in this cli-mate takes lots of work! So does keeping yourself clean. The need for three showers in 24 hours is not unusual in summer. Basically, every-thing takes more time, lots more time. What with the company, fam-ily, tourists, laundry, cooking, house, yard, special projects, pets, vol-unteer work, self-improvement and travel – all requiring much more time – I haven't the vaguest idea how I could possibly have a career

134

here. What do I DO here? I DO a lot. And, actually, I have NEVER spent a day under a palm tree drinking rum swizzles.

CHARM PLOWT

Five hundred years from now, some extraterrestrials are going to dig down deep and discover my diary. I wonder if they will ever discover what the circled letters C-H-A-R-M-P-L-O-W-T on every page mean? I'd better bury a copy of *Tea with Tracey* somewhere.

About the five-year point, I began to question myself. I have always maintained that if three people, totally unrelated to each other, tell me the same thing, I should think seriously about the validity of their statements. For example, if three friends tell me the colour of my dress is not quite right, I must assume that orange is not my colour. The dress must go. If three guests tell me an extra lamp in the cottage would be helpful, it's time to invest in another lamp and so on. This, to me, is the greatest gift one can give another – an honest appraisal. These are always difficult to relate; constructive criticism often provokes defensive behaviour. It takes courage. I admire this. I try to remember that one comment is simply opinion but, three similar remarks deserve serious attention. In the case of friends, I feel they are duty-bound to help me improve my lot and I feel the same responsibility towards them. I have never been accused of mincing words.

I had many discussions with strangers, friends and acquaintances. The same topics were always coming up: boredom, loneliness, nothing to do, monotony. I began to wonder why I was not having these problems. Was I the only person NOT bored, lonely, depressed? If so, why? (This is what happens when one has lots of reflection time. You think about the most ridiculous things – like, why you don't have problems!) I spent the next month researching this.

For the next 31 days, I recorded exactly what I did during every 24-hour period. I noted everything, and I mean everything. This was a pain in the neck – I spent as much time recording as I did "doing", but I had a mission. What I found after tabulating the results (which in itself took another month) was that 75% of my time was spent on five and ten minute chores. Hundreds of them, everyday: unload the

135

dishwasher, feed the chickens, load the dishwasher, chase a dog out of the yard, handwash the pots, take out the garbage, make the bed, feed the cats, change the kitty litter, get the mail, empty the dehumidifier, brush my teeth, answer the phone, rescue a chick, brush my hair, wash my face, shave, take the meat out of the freezer, make some milk, make some iced tea, put a new jug of water in the fridge, give the cats their flea pills, brush the cats, get dressed, open windows, close windows, make a pot of tea, make lunch, use the washroom, write in my diary, wash the fruit and on and on and on. This, then, only allowed 25% of the day for any major housework, cooking, laundry, reading, attention to myself, projects, purchasing groceries or shopping, exercise, planning and all the rest. Now THIS did seem ridiculous. Okay, I had identified the problem. Step two: find a solution.

I surmised that most daily work fell into ten main categories. I decided that I was prepared to give each category one hour. This would pretty well take care of the day but allow some time for other pursuits and the unexpected. By taking the first letter of each category, I came up with two words "charm" and "plowt". These expand to: cooking, housework, animals, reading, me, projects, laundry, out, walk and tidy. If I gave each of these one hour a day, I would accomplish everything I expected of myself. My home would be in order, meals would not be thrown together, the animals would be attended to, laundry would be up-to-date, there would be at least an hour for culture and exercise and out-of-the-house pursuits. This would also allow five hours a week towards a special project: furniture refinishing, shining silver, cleaning cupboards etc. I was quite impressed with this set-up. I still use it daily. It's especially helpful when I feel snowed-under.

Several accomplishments came out of this exercise. I now possessed the knowledge of – the answer to – "What do you DO here?" I found out, exactly, what I do here. I no longer wondered where the day went, where the time went. I knew that at least ten hours a day, I was active in positive pursuits. And I now controlled this situation. Being in control, this is important. This system also put a halter on one of my main character flaws – the inability to maintain balance and moderation. Results-oriented, I attack the job at hand with passion. Yes, this is also a good quality, but, in my case, it's excessive. I must constantly strive to put the brakes on. I don't refinish one piece of furniture, I do twenty. I don't write one letter, I write a dozen. I don't wash one wall, I wash fifteen. The results of this are strains and pains and the constant, depressing reminder that I'm not 20 years old anymore. It also makes it extremely difficult for others to work with me – I expect the same of them. I recognize this flaw and, as you can see, I DO work at stabilizing it. "Charm plowt" helps me do this.

The moral of this story: take control. Isolate your problems, identify them and find a way to solve them. Try this method to find out WHO you really are and WHAT you really want and WHY you don't have it. Positive, constructive, enlightening and fascinating – what could possibly be more interesting than an *exposé* of YOU!

Of course, this is only my opinion – you've only heard it once. Tell you what, read it three times and consider it fact.

POPE

The Pope lives in Hollywood.

There were a dozen reasons why I felt relocation to Bermuda would be a positive step forward. The reputation for excellence in the education system was one of them. Installation in this system was not, in itself, a guarantee of results. As with all worthy goals, there was a mountain to climb.

This was not an easy task for either of my children. They were in different schools; they were years behind. Both Paul and I were determined. Cassy and Scott were going to climb this mountain if we had to CARRY THEM UP. Scott's project on Bermuda's Open Spaces nearly killed me. Paul, brilliant as he is, had to bring the last twenty years of biology discoveries into his brain. For three years, from 7 till 10 p.m., five nights a week, the television and the telephone were off limits, for all of us. This was the time we tutored our children. It worked. Both kids graduated from high school, were accepted into Canadian universities and gained employment in the field of their choice.

The ascent up this mountain began the night Cassy asked me to test her for an upcoming quiz in history. I found this subject fascinating. She didn't. Her marks reflected this. I was contemplating how to go about transferring some of my enthusiasm to her very bored brain. I knew something had to be done, I just wasn't sure what. Her response to my first question (bound to be on the quiz) confirmed it. There was no more time to think; it was time for action.

My question was: "Where does the Pope live?" Her answer: "Well, he's famous ... I guess he must live in Hollywood."

From these humble beginnings, Cassy, her school and I brought a 48% History mark to 92. This was a great day. We proved she could do it. We showed her how. Now you have the time to make this type of investment in your children; the dividends will be concrete and far-reaching. A great school is only Step one.

How did I enhance her enthusiasm? Well, for one thing, I made a point of taking each history test myself. This created competition. Because mothers are expected to know everything, I had to get it right and to do that I had to study just as hard as Cassy and I HAD to receive a better grade. Paul insisted. We heard it so often, we all had it memorized. These were (and still are) his words: "No mark below an "A" is permitted at *Casscott.*" When taking a computer course, five years later, these words still haunted me. I passed the course. My mark was an "A". One will rise to the level of expectation. Expect a lot.

FAMILY

May 1966

Grandma asked me what I learned at school today. I told her biology was pretty interesting; we were studying a fruit fly, *Drosophila melanogaster.* Her reply: "Oh yes, I knew him once, poor soul, lost his wife you know, in the fire of '32, never was the same after that ...." This went on for two hours!

In the fast pace of the rat race, we often neglect and take for granted that which we value most highly. Bermuda has the tendency to put priorities in order. Leaving home intensely increases the appreciation for family. Now is an excellent time to turn your attention to those both in Bermuda and abroad.

Hopefully, you and yours have computers and can e-mail but, if not, write letters! If you don't send them, you won't receive them. You just won't be able to get enough news from back home. Now that you have the time, invest in a computer and learn the e-mail program. If remembering birthdays and special occasions has not been your forte up to now – start. Send cards, little notes and spend some time shopping for gift items to take with you when you go back to visit. Be wary of the telephone. Although rates have come down significantly, long distance calls can still break your budget. Write. There's something about sitting down with a letter and a cup of tea; there's something about putting your thoughts on paper. A letter is a gift of your own creation; uniquely yours, its value is priceless. How many priceless gifts can you give? Many, if they're letters! My family saves my letters. Mom, for instance, has documentation of my life since 1968! One day, some extraterrestrial ... .

It was Cassy's seventeenth birthday. She and Paul had spent the month struggling over her Spanish course (she didn't like this subject either). I wanted to do something special to break the tension, reduce the stress. She had requested a Midori cake. Midori is a liqueur made from honeydew melon. More research! I made the cake. I also bought six little gifts, wrapped them artistically and hid them all over the house. Then, I wrote out the clues on how to find them. The clues were in Spanish.

Do new and different things with and for your family while you're here. They will be gone all day giving you lots of time to plan and execute good meals and complete your chores before they arrive. There's time to take a walk with your hubby after supper. There's time to see what the kids learned today and to help them in any way you can. Be involved, be concerned, be a bigger part of their lives than time allowed in the past. Make a big splash of special events. Decorate the dining room for birthdays, wrap ten little gifts individually, make a flower arrangement for the table, prepare an exotic meal, a fancy cake. Plan a game of charades, a scavenger hunt. Prepare a smorgasbord, a salad bar, a picnic.

Remember the pets. What with the new sights, sounds and smells, this move is like landing on another planet for them. Give them lots of love and attention. Spend an hour bathing or brushing the dog and cat. Discuss the state of the world with them – they'll be ever so attentive.

You get what you give. Give lots!

VISITORS

Visitors from abroad bring days of beaching, sightseeing, relaxing and two new roles for you: tour guide and hostess. This is a constructive break in routine – you, too, take the time to smell the flowers, walk along the beach, take a dip in the ocean or try a new restaurant. Visitors are fun, exciting, enlightening and good for you. However, a few cautions are in order.

Recognize that you CANNOT put three gourmet meals on the table while you do the laundry, clean the house, and act as tour guide. You'll last about two days. I have a day in, day out concept that I work with. Guests can, of course, go out every day, but I need every second day to deal with the groceries, washing, ironing, housework (the yucky stuff). I also need some time to plan where we're going next. Guests don't have a problem with this. Often, they too would like some time alone or the opportunity to just read a book, suntan, sleep in or chit-chat. It makes a much more relaxing time for all. It took me five years to learn this.

For "out" days, this is a good plan: one day in Hamilton, one in St. George's, one in Somerset, one on the beach. This allows plenty of time for a bus ride to St. George's, a ferry ride to Somerset, leisurely lunches overlooking the harbour in town or a picnic in Par-la-Ville Park. It also allows for walks down the railway trails or along the beaches, a few hours of wandering around the larger hotels and perhaps having afternoon tea or shopping while there. The prices in the hotel shops are the same as in Hamilton – an excellent way to avoid the bustle of town if your guests are elderly, strapped for time, needing a last minute gift or just for a change of scenery. Be sure you have *This Week in Bermuda* or *Preview* as informational guides for guests. They're invaluable and free at the shops, hotels and tourist bureaus as are many other leaflets and brochures.

You will have visitors. Many of them. As the saying goes, "You don't know how many friends you have until you move to Bermuda." People who couldn't afford to go round the block will arrive on your doorstep. Caution: be selective with your invitations. It is quite possible to be at the airport, dropping off one set of guests and driving home with another. I don't recommend this. You need organization time. Guests are a lot of work no matter how compatible or how much you love them. If it's a two-year contract you're working on and everyone knows it, they will all try to get here within that time frame. If your friends and family number in the dozens, you're going to be a very busy (and cranky) lady. Remember, in between all this company, you too will be travelling and recuperating from that.

Too much company has not been a problem for me. I have a small family. Most of *my people* are so far away, it takes a year's planning just to get them down here. We also have a guest cottage so extra bedrooms and space are available. However, several of my acquaintances have had no end of grief over this. One of the braver souls has solved her problem in this way: when friends call to advise they are coming, she says, "Wonderful! I know this great little guest house. I'll call right now and book you in."

FRIENDS

Before I left Canada, I decided I had too many friends. (The goodbyes were a killer!) Friends require time, attention and love. You must see them often enough to stay in touch with their world and keep them up-to-date on yours. I am not referring to acquaintances here, I'm talking about friends. If you take these relationships seriously and be the best friend you can be, you can't have more than a few at any one time. I had a new husband, a new home and a new country to deal with. I promised myself I would NOT make a dozen new friends. I've kept that promise. It's easy in Bermuda.

The transient nature of the population here does not allow the accumulation of too many friends. Saudi Arabia, Spain, Kuwait, Italy and Wales are now home to some of my favorite "Bermuda" pals. We would have to take a year's sabbatical just to visit them all! Many of the ladies you will meet will be on a two- or three-year contract which may be half over before your first encounter. Keep this in mind if it's your tendency to get attached. You will always be saying goodbye. But, for heaven's sake, don't let this stop you! We all need a confidante, a buddy, a pal. This will be the person you whine and complain to. If you're lucky enough to make friends with a real

Bermudian, keep this in mind: this is their country, THEIR home – don't insult them by constantly grumbling about Bermuda.

As soon as you can, I recommend that you contact New Islanders. This is a division of The International American Women's Club that deals specifically with – you got it – new islanders. They will invite you to all sorts of events, include you in any group whose interests parallel yours, introduce you to all sorts of people and help you learn lots. No, you do NOT have to be American to join. I was here eight months before I found out about them. By then, I was definitely in need of a friend! Do give them a call, check it out, get involved. This will get you going and open up many opportunities. The women you will meet are in the same boat so you can even complain freely, if that's what you need to do. One way to meet twenty possible friends at one go!

If you have celebrated birthday 55, you are eligible to join another large, dynamic, friendly organization called The Seniors Learning Centre. Members attend (and teach) a wide variety of classes, seminars, activities and field trips. For additional information, contact the Bermuda College – the sponsor of this non-profit group.

One caution here. (Why is there always a caution?) Once you begin meeting people and getting involved, you'll find that time starts slipping away. Be wary of overextending yourself. It seems to be the tendency to jump into everything that comes along. Within six months, you'll be exhausted. There is so much to DO here, so many organizations that would like your help, so many clubs and so many ladies who would love to have your company that you can get snowed under! (Quite a feat in Bermuda, eh?) Be strong enough to say no when you feel this is happening. Too much is no better than too little. Moderation in everything.

VOLUNTEER

It was a plea suffused with passion, "You MUST come, we NEED you, DESPERATELY!" I had no idea who this woman was. I still don't and I'm certain she doesn't remember me. But I went. That was in 1987. I'm still there.

This little ditty illustrates several important points. One: a personal call works. Two: a passionate plea works wonders. Three: this "saleslady" should have received an award. Remember this story when you need something badly. It works.

This phone call began my "career" in volunteer work. I had received several letters from this organization asking for help, but letters like this were coming all the time. Basically, for no justifiable reason, I just ignored them. I didn't ignore the phone call.

The first time was an exercise in confusion – so many women, so much stuff, so much work – I couldn't imagine how many "woman hours" it took to put this together. It couldn't possibly be worth it! It was. It had been ... for 40 years.

Forty years ... this piece of information gained my instant respect and began a process of serious thought. Should I incorporate this charity into my life? I weighed it out. This work only went on two months a year. In those two months, I could come and go as I pleased – there were no schedules. If we were travelling, it wouldn't be a problem. I didn't need to make a commitment, buy special clothes or attend meetings. More thought brought more insight. The mission, the theory and the result meshed with everything I had been preaching for decades: the value of a hard day's work, of education, of discipline, of recycling. More thought. It bubbled to the surface. I HAD to do this. I OWED it. I could make some payments. That sealed it.

A hundred years' work couldn't repay this debt, but I could give it my best shot. The beneficiary of this charity had made a scholar of not only my husband but also my son. The beneficiary was Warwick Academy. The charity was The Clothing Mart.

Twice a year, Spring and Fall, these ladies put together a consignment sale of monumental proportions. I put in a consignment myself. This is a great exercise. First, it ensures that I clean my cupboards and closets twice a year (*keep it clean*). Secondly, it regularly disposes of goods I am not using (*keep it moving*). Thirdly, I receive a cheque for the goods sold. Great stuff! On sale days, the workers get first dibs on the merchandise. I have a ball – shopping! Basically, I'm exchanging useless items for useful ones – at no cost to me. Recycling at its finest!

Watch the newspapers in March and October and come on down to shop or to work. It's fun!

COMMUNITY SERVICE

I explained to our newly arrived English guests that I'd love to chat, but I simply had to go – I was late for my community service work. Little did I know that their connotation of this phrase meant I had been convicted of some crime and the judge had imposed a community service sentence. Apparently, in England, this is the only meaning of *community service*. It was some time before I got that straightened out! It's tough being global.

I like to think of community service as mandatory. It isn't but it should be. A gift we give Bermuda. A gift we give the world. A gift we give ourselves. In a country so small, the results are apparent and astounding.

Do it for yourself, do it for others, just do it. For purely selfish reasons you should do it. You must meet many people. You need to meet twenty women to find one *suitable* as a friend. In Bermuda, there are not many places you will find twenty women together in one place. But, they're there, in community service. It will give you a reason to get up and get going, especially if your hubby travels or you're childless. You will sleep better because there was a purpose to today – you did a good turn, you learned something. Even an hour will do this for you!

Do it for others. In every field, volunteers are needed. Whatever your problems, someone is worse off than you. It's good to be reminded of this on a regular basis. Whatever your particular interests are, there's a niche for you to fill. Plants, animals, children, the elderly, the mentally challenged, the physically challenged, the ill, the addicted – all need your help. For both men and women, the theatre is a popular choice (onstage or backstage) and obviously, it is a good place to meet a future date or mate! Perhaps the environment or the schools or politics ... whatever, it's here. Try half a dozen, see which ones are most enjoyable and satisfying. Use your talents; nourish your soul.

Classics

I walked back and forth, from the kitchen to the dining room, placing chicken, potatoes, green beans, salad, buns, gravy, water, tea and peach pie on the table for supper. The sight of all this food disgusted me. When Scott sat down and said, "When are we going to have beef?", that did it. I exploded.

This was the year I read the classics. My entire crew was happy to see that year end.

Concerned that my mind was turning to mush, I decided to take steps to ensure I was getting some culture – some mentally stimulating ideas, some intelligent food for thought. Something NOT related to babies or banana bread. I decided a leisurely, inexpensive way to accomplish this goal was by reading – a book a month, twelve a year – on topics I knew little about. The topic for the first year was Bermuda.

Three times a day I was running to the encyclopedia to look up something or another. So, the second year, I decided to learn a little about everything by reading the encyclopedia. At the conclusion of that year, I calculated that at the rate I was going, it would take 22 years to finish. Good grief. Year Three was upon me, it was time to choose another topic.

Year Three: the classics. This year was ever so enlightening. The two centuries preceding this one were not fun times. Seventy-five percent of the population fell victim to disease, starvation, war, torture and death long before their time. I had always been intensely grateful for what I had. I taught my children to end their nightly prayers with, "Thank you, Lord, for a warm house to live in, good food to eat and people to love us." When I looked out the window on cold winter nights, I said this prayer myself. These novels heightened this appreciation to monumental proportions. Our evening meal became an exercise in greed. Known for speaking my mind, I didn't keep these thoughts to myself. Any complaint on how "tough" things were was met with a diatribe of examples of how tough things could be: "Is anyone shooting at you? Has your mother been raped? Father tortured? Brother rotting in jail? Sister dying of consumption? Have you eaten in the last week? Had new shoes in the past five years?", and so on. *The magnitude of your problems is determined by the magnitude of your problems.* Needless to say, everyone was quite relieved to realize Year Four was upon us and the topic had changed to the best sellers.

The moral of this story? When you're bored, lonely, depressed – escape, step into another world by way of a book. Try reading about the problems others face. Chances are, you'll find you've got it pretty good.

HUGS

Go out and hug a tree.

For the last few years, I've been concentrating on another quest. I'd like to get to the bottom of this mind-over-matter business. If we're only using 10% of our brain, what in the world is the other 90% doing? I'm going to find out. At present, it appears I'll be able to answer this in ... oh ... about ... fifty years.

The knowledge of the universe is within us. We just don't know how to tap it. Life in Bermuda brings us one step closer. You will find yourself: gazing at the ocean ... wiggling your toes in the sand ... inspecting a leaf ... playing in the dirt. I'm not yet convinced that hugging a tree will solve the world's problems but, just in case, I'll do my part and give it a go.

Try to spend some of your time getting back to nature. Go back to childhood – play. Visualize pictures in clouds, watch ants at work, pick out the constellations. Because we are no longer savages, running naked through the jungle, we've lost touch with the wonder around us, with what's really important. Our universal knowledge is still there – buried, waiting. Now you have the time ... the opportunity ... the environment. Nurture it. That's what I'm trying to do. Nourish my soul. Perhaps, on your island travels, you'll see me. I'll be the one ... hugging the tree.

MEN, MOMS & SINGLES

Well. This is a fine how do you do. Due to popular demand, I now find myself writing on three lifestyles I've never even lived. I've never been single or a new mom in Bermuda. AND, I've never been a man anywhere. So ... would one of you fellows PLEASE end the aggravation and write the most requested, as yet unwritten, *Beer with Barney*? Honestly, I just haven't got the material, never mind the SOUL of the matter. At least I HAVE been single and a new mom at some point in this lifetime.

Being single in Bermuda has its advantages. You only have yourself to worry about. This means you do not have to listen to the daily whimperings of your unemployed spouse. This is a biggy. You are employed. This provides a team of people to help you out and answer your dozen questions a day. But, alas, nothing's perfect. It's lonely. Overcoming loneliness involves being with people. Go to everything you hear about. You may find you have interests you weren't aware of. If you are missing a certain club or organization from back home, see if there is a branch here. If not, start one. This happens all the time. Unfortunately, due to contracts expiring these groups stop as abruptly as they begin. A lady from Louisiana started a singles group and I sent her every single I met. But, her contract expired and she left. Perhaps you could fill her spot. If you're skipping all over this book instead of reading it front to back, read my section on Community Service and do all that too!

As a result of our guest business, I often meet single new residents and have opportunities to chat with them. Doug was brought in on a two-week contract. Each day he left for work at 7 a.m. and returned at midnight. At one point he mentioned that he wanted a wife. I told him that was never going to happen with the office hours he kept. Yes. Well. The following year I ran into him at the airport. He was now a husband. He explained that when he left our house to return to the States, he met a Bermudian lady on the plane. She is now his wife. Never say never.

Cassy, living in Halifax at the time, was between boyfriends. Having nothing exciting on her plate and with the direct flight to Bermuda on sale, she thought she would just pop home and see mom. Kids tend to do that when they lose a mate. Anyway, she arrived to tell me she had a Bermuda dinner date with a Haligonian. Pretty sad when one has to get on a plane to Bermuda to get a date with a guy from Halifax. I'm beginning to think there would be far fewer marriages without airplanes.

Steve, a positively gorgeous chap, was brought in as a salesman. Within a few months, the female population was abuzz over him. There was no question about it; he was not hurting for companionship. After he found his own apartment, I had a call from a lady who wanted to have tea with Tracey. It was his long-time girlfriend from Boston. Great. Now *what* was I supposed to do? The only way she could have known about me was through Steve. He had left us months before so HE must have given HER my phone number. What, on earth, was his intention here? He couldn't have known I was aware of his reputation with the ladies. Why would he want me to talk to her? Keep in mind that I had exactly one minute to process all of this. Basically, I said, "Okey dokey." Yikes, HOW do I get into these things? Anyway, while she was making her way over here, I had ten minutes to think. I decided I would volunteer no information, but would ask pertinent questions leading her to her own conclusions. And yes, her question was, "Should I move to Bermuda and marry Steve?" So, I asked her: How often does *he* call *you*? Whose idea was it for you to come for a visit? How often has *he* initiated the discussion of your future? Whose idea was marriage? And so forth. After several hours of this soul-searching, the answer was clear. What I'm certain her subconscious knew all along had now been coaxed to the surface. She was hurt. I didn't feel bad; I felt relieved. I just couldn't see this beautiful, sensitive, loving lady dumping her job, her life, her country and moving here to marry a man obviously not ready for that. I don't know what happened to her, but Steve ended up marrying a European woman whom he has since divorced. So ... if you're looking for a mate, a date, an escape or a European, Bermuda may be just the place for you!

Now, new moms have this date business all sorted out, but they have other problems. Notice how you never actually get away from problems – all you ever do is trade one set for another. This is maturity: *knowing* there's always a choice, *knowing* every choice has problems and *knowing* which set you'd rather deal with! Oops ... sorry ... I got off track there ... which reminds me of the oops story ... okay, okay, I'll pay attention .... New moms have lost their support group.

Parents, friends and babysitters have been left behind. Freedom is a lost concept. So, what they must do now is begin again. The best way to meet new moms is at the playground and the beach. Dad can benefit from these excursions too. The word I've received: this is a great way to network. Other dads are there, babysitting too, and would really appreciate a stimulating conversation on the merits of Version 9.0 of some computer program, the Somerset cricket team and such. The adults at the playground are parents; they have the same concerns as you; they can babysit for you; they can tell you what they've learned, accompany you to kids' events and provide a playmate for your little tyke. *Talk to them!*

Conclusion

Everything is relative. It must be remembered that your country too has its problems. Friends abroad report taxes, unemployment, floods, crime, blizzards, pollution, poisonous snakes and dust storms are driving THEM crazy. Personally, I think earthquakes must be particularly scary; with the others, at least you're on solid ground. On the tough days, try to remember why you wanted to come to Bermuda in the first place. I had a list of twelve goals this move was to achieve. Mission accomplished. Yes, all twelve. Try to think of those things you would miss if you left. There are many. Bermuda-made friends, now relocated, continually remind me of this. Last and most importantly, try to keep things in perspective. Bermuda is not a hardship posting.

If you are new to the island or contemplating a move here, please, please, please give Bermuda time to work her magic on you. Every great accomplishment, every major adjustment requires time. The ladies who lasted one month, three months – didn't give it time. You must allow yourself the experience of each season. One year is simply the minimum length of time for a major adjustment such as this. You cannot make an intelligent decision under the inevitable stress this year will bring. Then, if you still want to leave, go home for a holiday first. You will find the world you left behind has changed, you have changed. This is inevitable; the only constant is change. Many have come, left and come back again. An expensive lesson to learn both financially and emotionally.

You have now heard MY trials and tribulations, and the results of my YEARS of research. As you've probably gathered, this was not an easy adjustment for me. But, I was not held prisoner. Paul stated, from the outset, that he could live anywhere and be happy. Actually, I'm certain he would be thrilled to be posted to Australia! Of course, I would follow him anywhere, but for me – my personal, individual, selfish little self, I'd rather stay ... in paradise.

Recommendations

When we arrived, there was no television. There had been, but a strike shut it down. The last movie theatre had just closed. Finding a pizza after 10 p.m. was an exercise in frustration. Sales were few and a 15% reduction was a big deal. Now, pizza is not only available, but delivered; we have three television stations (plus cable) and four movie theatres. Half-price sales abound and ethnic restaurants have arrived and flourished.

I *really, really, really* want to tell you about my favourite spots – to eat, to drink, to shop, to have a great cup of coffee – you know, the fun stuff. BUT, I've been down this road twice (with two printings) AND in person. I can tell you, it's a dead end. I'm reminded of a trip we took to Greece. We spent an entire day taking taxis to non-existent laundromats. They were all listed in our *updated* tourist guide but they weren't there anymore. I was REALLY cranky. I'm not going to do this to you. Bermuda is a happening place; dreams are realized, then abandoned. There's money here. This allows creation on a whim and closure in a heartbeat. As the old folks retire and the kids pursue their own agendas, even the businesses that have been around *forever* are not a safe bet. My best advice: TALK to people. In this country, it's easy. Both Bermudians and ex-pats WANT to be helpful. This is how it's done: make eye contact, say "Good morning", smile, and away you go.

Try to read the newspaper first thing in the morning. Many sales and events are not advertised until the day they are happening. I find this most frustrating as Paul brings the paper home from work each day. By the time I've seen the ad, it's over. (For all you advertisers out there, I, for one, need a little more notice if you'd like to get my dollar, attendance, etc.) Be sure to check *The Bermuda Calendar* section for an exhaustive list of all the goings-on in this tiny little place.

I highly recommend the magazine called *The New Residents Guide* – the name says it all. And, if you are interested in plants, animals, fish and a zillion other things, call the Ministry of the Environment and ask to be put on the mailing list for their monthly bulletin called *Environtalk*. It's free. I've been receiving it for more than a decade. One reason why I know all this stuff!